BUILDING BRANDS
BUILDING MEANING

BUILDING BRANDS BUILDING MEANING

A guide to increasing the financial value of brands through building positive meaning

Kartikeya Kompella

Viva Books Private Limited
New Delhi • Mumbai • Chennai • Kolkata • Bangalore • Hyderabad

First Published 2006

VIVA BOOKS PRIVATE LIMITED

- 4737/23, Ansari Road, Daryaganj, New Delhi 110 002
  Tel. 42242200, 23258325, 23283121 E-mail: vivadelhi@vivagroupindia.net
- Plot No. 76, Service Industries, Shirvane, Sector 1, Nerul, Navi Mumbai 400 706
  Tel. 27721273, 27721274 E-mail: vivamumbai@vivagroupindia.net
- Jamals Fazal Chambers, 26 Greams Road, Chennai 600 006
  Tel. 28294241, 28290304 E-mail: vivachennai@vivagroupindia.net
- B-103, Jindal Towers, 21/1A/3 Darga Road, Kolkata 700 017
  Tel. 22816713 E-mail: vivakolkata@vivagroupindia.net
- 7, GF, Sovereign Park Aptts., 56-58, K. R. Road, Basavanagudi, Bangalore 560 004
  Tel. 26607409 E-mail: vivabangalore@vivagroupindia.net
- 101-102, Moghal Marc Apartments, 3-4-637 to 641, Narayanguda, Hyderabad 500 029
  Tel. 27564481 E-mail: vivahyderabad@vivagroupindia.net

http://www.vivagroupindia.com

ISBN 81-309-0339-3

Published by Vinod Vasishtha for Viva Books Private Limited,
4737/23 Ansari Road, Daryaganj, New Delhi 110 002.

Printed & bound by Sanat Printers, Kundli, Haryana.

To Kireeti, Vach and Vinitha

Contents

Preface

OUR LIVES are dominated by brands. We work for brands, we buy brands, we invest in brands, our life savings are deposited in a brand that gives a 3 per cent rate of interest, etc. With brands playing such an all-pervasive role in our lives, it is understandable that brands can influence us in many ways.

The financial misdemeanours of a handful of brands made stock markets across the world go into a downward spiral. Many lost jobs, others lost their lifetime savings. In another scenario, there are people struggling in a loveless work life, confused and frustrated because of a lack of direction at work, hating the company that they work for. Elsewhere consumers are delighted at the fact that they can fly at an extremely low cost enabling them to visit their loved ones because of an airline that has the vision to help them and does so in a warm and friendly manner. Brands can cause happiness or sorrow, build or destroy, depending on what they want to do and how they are run.

When brands can play such an important role in our lives, it is only smart to leverage the power of these brands in every way possible. Running a brand to ensure that it delivers value and profits in both the short and long term is a business function. Brands can operate as strong businesses and also use their power to improve people's lives.

In fact, these two functions go hand in hand because the better the brand behaves towards its constituents, the better it is for its brand equity. Stronger brand equity delivers better sales, and if the business is soundly run, the profits are better.

Strong brands derive more than just the business benefits of higher sales, but also a lot of hidden savings through employee and associate loyalty, better quality manpower availability, trade support, etc. Brands that act in an insensitive and unethical manner can lose these hidden savings very quickly as word goes out against the brand.

It is stupid and extremely bad business sense for brands to ignore the many business benefits that ethical, sensitive behaviour towards their constituents can earn the brand. Unfortunately, at times brand custodians are afflicted by greed, ignorance and myopia that leads them to hurt brand equity whilst in the pursuit of short-term gains.

There is a chance for brands to make money while making the world a better place for all those they interact with and I hope that more and more brands will work in this direction.

I would like to thank the different people who gave me feedback as I was trying to form my ideas on branding – Simon Anholt, Chris Macrae, Tom Blackett, Ramesh Jude Thomas, Philip Cross, John Moore, Priya Raghubir, Jonas Bergvall and Tom Asacker, all of whom, at some point of time, gave me advice or encouragement. A special mention must be made of Chris Macrae, who encouraged me to write this book.

Special thanks to www.brandchannel.com for allowing me to reproduce in this book modified versions of my articles 'Brand Intent' as well as 'Your Brand's Heritage May Hold the Keys to Its Future', which originally appeared on the Brandchannel site. Thanks also to Ren Spiteri of VirtualBulldog, on whose site www.virtualbulldog.com, an earlier version of my chapter 'Concern Goes a Long Way' first appeared.

Many thanks to Pabitra, Richa, Amod, Shrijit, Satish Chandra, Rahul, JC and Jatinder for their inputs in terms of proof checking, editing, designing and production.

Last but not the least I would like to thank my wife and mother for putting up with my prolonged preoccupation with writing this book.

I hope you enjoy this book and find it useful. All the opinions expressed here are mine and do not reflect the opinions of my organisation. Do mail me your feedback and suggestions at kartik@buildingbrandmeaning.com.

1

Branding for Business

BRANDING IS the most powerful business tool available today. Some people feel that branding is marketing blah blah backed by advertising jargon. However, branding has moved well beyond the marketing function to demonstrate its overall role in building strong businesses. Interbrand's valuation of the world's biggest brands clearly demonstrates in business terms the huge financial value that branding can provide an organisation.

Brands have value because they mean something to their constituents – consumers, trade, employees, associates, investors, et al. The more powerful the meaning, the greater the brand equity and the higher the value of the brand. Coke represents America, and because it stands for such a powerful concept, it has become the brand with the highest valuation in the world.

Building brands is all about building meaning, and this obviously is more than just a marketing task. This is an organisational task that stems from the very purpose of the organisation. Wipro is not a marketing wonder; it is an organisational wonder, because it lives its purpose and reflects this in all that it does.

To create a deep resonant meaning, brands need to live what they stand for, thereby letting all their constituents experience the meaning that the brand represents. All that a brand says or does reinforces the existing meaning or adds new meaning to the brand. Brand meaning can be tainted or even eroded if there is a dissonance between its significance and its actions. If a brand uses outsourced sweatshops to get its products manufactured at a low cost in order to boost profitability, then this act would give a negative meaning to the brand that negatively impacts its valuation.

Brands get several business benefits due to their equity, and the best way to maintain these benefits is by operating in a decent, caring manner with a clear, long-term view. To get a consistent focused message out, brands need to make everyone associated with them think and act in this focused manner, thereby reinforcing the meaning that the brand has.

Crude shortcuts only hurt the brand value by taking away the meaning of the brand. For example, if a toiletry brand that professes concern for one's skin suddenly starts using chemicals that can harm one's skin, then the meaning of the brand changes. The brand will lose the trust that consumers reposed in the brand, based on which the brand was consumed, and sales will plummet.

One measure of the strength of the brand is its valuation, which is a function of the brand's equity. Brand valuation reflects the health of the brand in financial terms depicting the value derived from owning the brand. This is determined through the brand's current earnings and its potential future earnings. Current and future earnings are a function of the brand's relationships and its meaning.

A variety of factors work towards increasing brand valuation. These range from the brand's relationship with trade to its ability to command a premium over competition to the quality of people working for the brand.

Brands need to focus on pushing their valuation higher as this is a sign of financial health. However, for a brand to have a truly enduring growth in brand valuation, it has to go beyond purely financial parameters. This is because the human element plays a vital role that is central to any brand whether it is in the form of the consumers' relationship with the brand or the employees' and associates' loyalty and commitment to the brand.

To be consistently successful brands need to have a proper mix of business and people perspectives, and brand valuation is a measure of not just the hard side of business but its softer side too. As many have found, it is possible to run an increasingly profitable business while maintaining ethics and humanity in their dealings. In fact this is the only way to run a successful sustainable business. Branding shows the direction for successful sustainable business practices, and brand valuation takes a beating when these practices are flouted.

To understand the relationship between running a business in a decent ethical manner, brands and valuation, one must understand what branding is all about. Branding is about brands providing a meaningful relationship to their constituents that has a commercial value. A relationship can take the form of liking, preference, a sense of trust, a belief in quality, etc. that leads the constituent to want to continue consuming the brand.

If there is no relationship with it, then an offering has only a name but is not a brand. Going by this definition, a much-advertised offering does not become a brand because of high awareness levels; only when the consumer develops a relationship with the offering does it become a brand.

However, the relationship created has to also have a commercial value. Constituents should be willing to pay a commercial value for maintaining the relationship and this is a good test of a brand. One can easily create habits with free products, and this can be mistaken for a relationship, but the proof of the relationship is the brand's ability to get a decent return on its transaction with the consumer.

Some of the several benefits that strong brands enjoy are listed below. It is never worth losing out on any of these for short-term benefits. This is a lesson that Enron and Arthur Andersen would be learning.

Drive those volumes consistently: A good brand sells a base consistent level of volumes in its market regularly. Whether it is Coke, Ariel, Samsung, Nirma or Revlon, these brands have a base consistency in terms of sales to consumers.

In these days of mass production and just-in-time supplies, it is important to ensure that there is a consistent base demand for the brand from consumers. This provides economies of scale and keeps costs under control.

Brands have a relationship with their consumers, and this relationship ensures that the consumers consistently consume the brand. In contrast, sales of unbranded products tend to fluctuate largely as a function of demand–supply economics.

Better profitability by commanding a premium: Strong brands are often able to get a premium over competition based on their brand equity. Often we find that consumers are willing to pay a few rupees more to buy a known brand instead of its not-so-well-known competitor. This explains why Tropicana can price its juice far higher than other lesser juice brands.

Brands build insurance against bad times: It is easy enough to forgive a friend for a mistake; however, it is not so easy to forgive a stranger for the same mistake. Similarly, consumers tend to be more forgiving towards known brands that have made a mistake than they would be towards unknown labels.

This is why strong brands that have had to pull back products due to existing or perceived flaws (Intel, Tylenol) have been able to recapture their consumers' faith without fading into obscurity. The strong relationship that these brands had with their constituents prevented them from dying the way mere labels would have.

Relationships often have tied up with them a past (with memories of good times or convenience), a present and an expected future. Customers who face problems with a brand often look at their past experiences with the brand and forgive the brand for a current problem as they also see the brand continuing to play a relevant role in their future.

Commands shelf space: Trade often favours big brands, and the majority of the extremely scarce shelf space is dedicated to big brands. Trade tends to accept less-favourable terms from big brands because the consistency of volumes of these brands gives them fairly large and regular earnings. A P&G would almost never have problems with getting adequate shelf space while a new label from an unknown company may not even manage to get shelf space.

The best talent: Big brands tend to get good manpower. Prospective employees flock to them for recruitment even though many big brands do not pay very well except in the senior positions. The task of getting high-quality manpower at fairly economical rates becomes easier for companies that are well known and respected. Employees of these brands tend to compensate themselves for slightly lower salaries with the security and the reflected aura of the brand that employs them.

No dearth of willing lenders: One of the less-discussed but extremely obvious advantages of a big brand is the relative ease with which it can raise money. Financiers would probably fight each other to be able to lend money to blue-chip companies like Cisco or Microsoft. Money comes to them easily either through public issue of shares or through loans repayable in attractive instalments. Financial institutions often are reassured by the strength of a borrowing brand's equity, and this often plays a large role in smoothening the loan-sanction process.

Claim to immortality: There is no telling the life of a label, but brands have long lives because of the relationships they enjoy and the values they represent. Some of the world's best-known brands are over a 100 years old. Coke, Pepsi, Quaker Oats and Jockey are but a few of these old but strong brands.

The following chapters will seek to show how being honest, decent and caring can help a brand reinforce its meaning, business and improve valuation.

2

Good Intent Makes for Good Business

THE STRENGTH of brands is a function of the strength of their intent. Intent is all about what the brand has come into existence to do. It is the brand's raison d'être. Intent infuses meaning into the brand. A hotel brand may be driven by the intent to give people staying away from home the comfort and joy of being at home; a health brand may be driven by the intent to make people lead happier lives by keeping them healthy and pain free.

The pharma company Merck explained their intent simply by stating that their intent is helping patients. Profits, they said, were only a by-product of the task of helping patients. Intent focuses on what the consumer gets and not what the brand gets. It is about consumer benefits, not investor benefits. The underlying belief is that if consumers are happy this will translate into investor benefits.

Intent forms the basis of the consumer–brand relationship. Consumers see the brand's intent and know what to expect. Intent directs the energies of the brand in the direction of the brand promise. It ensures that all systems and processes are directed towards making the brand perform what it promises. All systems and processes are geared towards delivering according to the brand intent. The synergy of systems and processes working towards a common goal enables consistency in the brand's image and delivery on the brand promise that is critical in ensuring the brand's longevity.

Intent is a function of strong-mindedness. It is not what the brand would like to do; it is what the brand is determined to do. It brooks no opposition and its force gives credibility to the brand promise and purpose to the organisation. A change in intent takes away the single-mindedness and focus of the brand and makes it fuzzy and weak.

Let's look at a power generation company that has a clear intent to provide power to make its consumers' lives more comfortable. The brand has excellent customer care and zero downtime. Suddenly the brand realises that it wants to make a lot of money, and it starts cutting corners. The company makes a small modification in its billing software that surreptitiously adds one unit to every hundred units consumed. To save money, the manpower in the customer care department is reduced and an automatic complaint registration software is put in place. Further cost cuts led to a lower number of service people handling the same number of complaints.

The result? Consumers who feel that their bill is a little higher than normal, but can't put a finger on what the problem is. Consumers who call the call centre find that they are greeted by an automated service rather than a friendly person. The service person who visits for repairs is under pressure because there are fewer people in the same department handling the same number of complaints. So the serviceperson is hurried, brusque and impersonal.

On each front the brand is losing out on its relationship with its customers and customers start shifting their business to a different power corporation. This is the beginning of the end of the brand as customers see that the brand's intent has changed from serving customers, to serving its own interests. Consequently, the brand loses its ability to retain those customers who entered into a relationship with the brand based on its earlier intent. Enron, Arthur Andersen and Tyco seem prime examples of brands that seem to have forgotten their original 'intent'.

Harley Davidson is a brand that virtually came back from the dead because of the sheer intent of its management. Ironically, the brand was a victim of its own success. The brand's success led it to keep increasing its production capacity and the intent shifted to serving its own needs (mass production) from serving customer needs (quality).

The onslaught of Japanese bikes and Harley's quality problems led to the brand losing market share from 43 per cent to less than 20 per cent. The brand's management that took over the company revitalised the brand by refocusing on the brand's intent and in the process re-ignited their customers' love for the brand.

Intent often is at its strongest when the brand's founder is at the helm. Walt Disney is an example of a brand that has always had a strong sense of clear intent linked to a set of values. As a person Walt Disney possessed a single-minded intent to provide the world with wholesome family entertainment. This sense of intent drove him to maintain high standards of delivery irrespective of the possible negative financial implications that this could have had on his business.

It is said that Disney once gave up a film half way through when he discovered a new technology, so that he could remake the film using a better technology, and in doing so, make the movie more appealing to its viewers.

Intent provides guidance when it comes to decision making. Whether to expand into a new area or not, whether to cut back on a particular service, whether to make or buy is evaluated against how these actions will impact the brand in the context of delivering according to its stated intent.

Intent is a strong advertisement for the brand. Apple's intent helped it attract thousands of high-quality employees. SouthWest's intent to make people's travel more affordable and enjoyable has made millions of people feel strongly for the brand. Intent shines through with credibility.

Intent is often confused with the brand's desire or want. The difference between 'wanting' and 'intending' is significant as the latter denotes the willingness to put effort behind the desire. Merck's willingness to first create a new product and then look at its profitability led them to manufacture MECTIZAN, which helps treat river blindness.

Merck did not find an immediate market for this product and hence went on to manufacture and distribute it to those afflicted with river blindness absolutely free with a commitment to continue distributing this for as long as necessary.

Brands that have a strong intent tend to overcome serious hurdles. Strong intent at times makes up for lack of resources. SouthWest Airlines sticking to their low-fares strategy despite facing severe financial problems is testimony of their strong intent.

Despite the benefits of strong intent in keeping a brand alive, it is not always easy for brands to maintain intent as it often means doing things the hard way and taking tough, unpopular decisions. If maintaining brand intent is not a part of the organisation's charter, then sooner or later the brand will run into trouble.

3

Differentiation – The Brand Lifeline

THE PRETTY FACE in the crowd, the jewel in the crown, the ugly duckling – all get noticed because they are different from the others. The mind cannot process the millions of stimuli that one comes into contact with on a daily basis and blocks out much of the stimuli; it notices only what is different from the regular. This is true of all things and brands are no exception. Ask any marketer – it takes differentiation for a brand to stand out.

The most important facet of any strong brand is the difference it provides from other offerings. It is impossible for a brand that is unnoticed to go on and build a relationship with its prospects and customers. Differentiation has been identified as the single strongest attribute of leading brands, as differentiation makes the brand noticeable and memorable.

As competition grows in any market, it gets increasingly tougher for a brand to get shelf space or mind space. With more and more brands targeting the same prospects through the same media and retail outlets, the task of being noticed and considered becomes exceedingly difficult for brands, and their attempts at blasting themselves into their audiences' consciousness is normally met by prospects mentally blocking out these brands.

While the importance of differentiation cannot be overemphasised, it is only 'relevant' differentiation that actually works. Nike's differentiation of being a 'successful, spontaneous, achievement-led' sports shoe is extremely relevant in the context of sports shoes worn largely by the youth. In the context of automobiles, the driving pleasure that BMW talks of is an important differentiator and is very relevant for wealthy people who love driving.

To be enduringly successful, differentiation has to be meaningful and while this may sound commonsensical, not all marketers realise this. Funky-looking furniture may look wildly different but will rapidly lose its charm if it is not comfortable; however, even plain-looking furniture that is ergonomically designed to provide extra comfort would provide differentiation that is meaningful to customers.

The same furniture in a more stylised version with the same ergonomic benefits at a higher price again offers a relevant 'differentiator' – this time in terms of the psychological satisfaction of being able to afford well-designed luxurious furniture.

Surprisingly, in a category like furniture that appears terribly staid and unexciting, there are a large number of differentiators possible. Victorian furniture, Chippendale furniture, contemporary stylised furniture, ergonomically designed furniture, DIY furniture and eco-friendly furniture are just some of the more obvious differentiators that brands have used to market themselves better.

There are successful furniture brands built around each type of differentiation. In fact, Ikea is a great example of a furniture brand that created a whole market through 'do-it-yourself' differentiation.

The enduring relevance of a brand's offering is what develops and ensures a lasting relationship, and this is the defining factor of any brand. If the differentiator loses its relevance with time, the brand will require to develop a new differentiator to grab customers' attention, and this often means that the brand is talking to a new set of customers and is creating a new relationship.

This is the tendency of a label and not a brand. Trying to build a brand on the basis of the differentiator that is not enduring is like building a sand house – a lot of hard work can get swept away pretty easily. This is seen in the case of fads – remember the days when people used to buy pet rocks? More recently, virtual pets had a large following for a while.

Brands need to recognise and protect their differentiation. New Coke was a failure possibly because it struck at Coke's differentiation of being the original Cola. A brand's positioning is derived from its differentiation, and the perceptual distance from one brand and another (which brands must try to maximise) is defined by the extent of differentiation.

Differentiation can be manifested in a variety of ways from pack size, pack shapes, pricing, service levels or even brand personality. Door delivery is Domino's differentiator, less filling is Miller Lite's differentiator, driving pleasure is BMW's differentiator and safety is Volvo's differentiator. As markets get increasingly saturated, it gets tougher to find an enduring differentiator. Paradoxically, the saturated market scenario is actually when brands need to have a really good differentiator.

Developing a relevant, meaningful, enduring differentiator does not come from having better machines, designers or software. It starts by the brand feeling differently towards their customers. For example, at SouthWest Airlines there is a heartfelt commitment to providing low-cost, high-quality flying services with a lot of entertainment thrown in. Brands need to recognise and believe in their differentiator and give it due support.

Recognising and believing in their differentiator is not as easy and commonsensical as it sounds. 7 Up's 'uncola' campaign gave them a clear differentiation from other soft drinks, but they did not seem to believe in this concept for long and soon changed what was a winning concept. They haven't been lucky enough to find a winner twice.

Brands have to create a culture where differentiation is allowed to foster and grow. Apple did this brilliantly in the early eighties where the Apple team thrived in an environment that provided them all the support to build something that was unique.

The process of creating and sustaining differentiation has to be built into the way the brand functions or else it becomes a forced differentiation and there will be lapses in consistency of the image. If a brand's differentiation is all about passion, then it cannot afford to have customer service or call centre personnel who lack passion. The brand needs to equip itself with resources who are attitudinally inclined towards living this differentiation.

Impressions are created through holistic synergistic efforts, and if some facets of the brand do not display the differentiation, then the overall image may get diluted. When employees are attitudinally in line with the brand and processes are in line with maintaining this differentiation, then brands are reasonably well protected from getting a diluted image.

Brands also need to put resources behind their differentiators as this is the driver of the brand image. If excellence in electronics and innovation are Sony's differentiators, then it is only wise to dedicate the best of the brand's resources towards constantly improving these facets rather than diverting the brand's focus towards activities such as cost cutting or developing greater manufacturing efficiencies.

For any brand it is important to put resources behind reinforcing its differentiation as this is one of its critical business drivers. Differentiation is a critical driver of brand valuation as it is the foundation of the brand relationship and brand equity.

It is important to be different and build a place in the consumer's mind, but then it is also equally important to remain different by using meaning to strengthen the brand's position in the consumer's mind for ever.

4

Values – The Cornerstone of Brand Relationships

VALUES ARE inherent to every individual. Values are developed on the basis of one's upbringing, social conditions and the individual's unique situation, etc. Values influence attitudes and beliefs. Values are central to an individual's life, and they determine behaviour.

In the context of branding, values play an important role. Brand meaning gets enhanced by the values that the brand possesses. Individuals tend to search for relevant values in the brands that they associate with. Brand values assume great importance in gaining customer acceptance and developing enduring relationships. As values are reasonably stable, they provide the basis for enduring relationships as long as the brands can deliver strongly on these values.

The values that individuals seek vary by purchase context. The Nike customer most likely would not bank with a bank that endorses the 'just do it' philosophy in its investments. The Rolls-Royce customer would probably demand economical pricing, power and superior performance if he had to buy trucks for his transport business.

The entertainment business has fascinating examples of how customers relate to different values. If The Beatles represented values of freshness, innocent rebellion and fun, Pink Floyd during the same era depicted experimental art rock and a bleak viewpoint of life. Many people listen to both forms of music relating to two distinctly different sets of brand values within the category of music.

Customers look at brands as baskets of values. The primary values are the values that drive the relationship. These values are differentiating values. The secondary values are values that are important but not critical to the relationship.

In a Volvo, safety is a primary value while fuel efficiency may be a secondary value. Fun, youth, wanting more are primary values depicted by Pepsi and drive the relationship. That it may have fewer calories than other colas may be seen as a secondary value amongst hardcore Pepsi drinkers.

There are times when secondary values need to move up the brand value scale. Diet Pepsi represented as having low calories is an important value as people become more health-conscious; similarly, economy is a value that may move from the secondary to primary category during a recession depending on the product category of the brand.

Brand equity is a function of constituents believing in the brand's ability to deliver on the values that are core to the customer. So if a customer wants safety, he/she will buy Volvo as long as Volvo stands for safety and manifests this better than other car brands. Monitoring brand equity is best done by constantly monitoring the brand's score on the core values vis-a-vis other brands in the same category as well as with generic competition.

This means it is important for Volvo to not only be seen as the safest car but also keep an eye out for generic competition that may at some time intrude onto its territory. Therefore it is important for Volvo to understand where it stands in the context of personal transport too. Tracking the brand on both parameters is critical as these indicate the strength of the relationship. The first parameter determines the strength of the relationship/brand differentiation, the second parameter determines the relevance of the brand at a category level.

Often customers are loyal to values more than they are to specific brands. So if Volvo stops meaning safety, then it is more than likely that customers seeking safety, rather than sticking on to Volvo, will move to another brand that offers safety.

Values determine the direction of brand extension that is possible and the extent of its probable success. The values and relationship show just how far the brand can be extended. Xerox, which stood for high-quality copying and document services, could not extend into computers because its values did not include innovation or tech savviness, which were critical values for computer companies. Disney stands for wholesome family entertainment and hence could be extended into comics, cartoons, theme parks, holiday resorts, etc., all of which reflect wholesome family entertainment.

While brand values are critical in the context of brand marketing, brands also need to look at their overall organisational values, for this determines the benefits to the brand as an organisation as well as impacts customer perceptions of the brand.

In addition to standing for a set of values vis-a-vis customers in the context of marketing, brands need to have values that are relevant to all their constituents. Brands need to have sound corporate values. They need to show honesty, integrity, fairness and other positive values that will help them attract the right employees, investors, suppliers and associates. Constituents will gravitate towards whatever they find relevant to their value system.

A brand that depicts values of stability of investment or work environment will be relevant to a set of investors and employees as opposed to another brand that depicts aggressiveness and constant change.

Just as brands may lose customers if they change their values, they may lose employees if they shift their values significantly.

Focusing on the core values and ensuring that they are being depicted well is the most important thing in branding as it is the basis of the relationship that the brand has with all its constituents.

5

The Price and Value Relationship

BRANDS CHARGE customers for buying their products or services. The price charged has several implications on the brand in terms of how it is perceived by customers, how it repositions other brands, how it influences demand, how it affects the profitability and revenues of the organisation and so on.

Based on the business objectives, market scenario and other factors, brands develop their pricing strategy. Timex's pricing helps the brand drive volumes. Virgin's economy-pricing strategy made competition look as though they provide less value for the money charged. Mercedes's premium pricing strategy makes less expensive brands seem inferior.

The importance of pricing cannot be overemphasised and brands need to understand what it is that customers are paying for when they buy a brand and how this influences consumer perceptions and the bottomline.

Customers buy values and emotional satisfaction manifested in the form of a particular product or service. Customers are willing to pay a particular price for a set of values in the context of a particular product or service category. This price would vary based on the blend of values and the manifestation offered by different brands.

Nike had identified a set of values such as spontaneity, passion, aggression; the preferred shoe of successful sports people and comfort that consumers would perceive to be relevant in the context of shoes. Nike's unique depiction of these values and consistency in communicating these values has led to consumers associating the brand with these values. The nature of these values and Nike's manifestation of these values has led consumers to be willing to pay a premium for Nike shoes.

Given that the price that a consumer is willing to pay is a function of the value that he mentally assigns to the brand, it is important to know exactly which values the consumer is willing to pay for. Once this is known, the next task would be to identify the maximum amount that the consumer would pay for the brand offering and devise plans to make the offering worthy of a higher price. To maximise the value that can be charged for a product or service, it is important to maximise the value in the consumers' mind.

Consumers buy offerings based on the values that the offering stands for. In the consumers' mind these values have a hierarchy, and each value has a monetary value attached to it. This gives cues as to the strengthening of which values would lead to the consumer being willing to pay a higher price for the brand.

The more the brand can teach the consumer to appreciate the brand's values the greater the chance of revenue maximisation. For example, a Levis customer may be paying for the product, fit, style, durability and heritage of the brand. If Levis were to know how much the customer is willing to pay for each of these facets of the offering, then it would know whether it is charging the right price for the brand and on what aspects it is overpriced or underpriced.

Importantly, the brand can understand the areas where a customer is willing to pay more. For example, if customers are buying Levis because it is the 'original' jeans, then the more customers get to experience the Levis heritage the more they feel for the brand, and this is where the brand may probably be able to charge a premium.

For a brand to be priced well, customers need to feel that they are getting good value for their money. Value for money does not mean low cost or inexpensive product – it means getting equal or more value from the brand than the amount paid.

For example, a cologne brand may charge $100 for its offering that is known to convey masculinity, confidence and style. The customer is paying for the feeling of masculinity, confidence and style and as long as these values are worth more than $100 to him and he feels that the brand is delivering these values to him better than other brands can, he will feel that the brand has given him good value for money.

To illustrate this point further take the case of BMW: While it is a high-priced car, few BMW owners complain of the price as they feel that they are getting good value for money.

Pricing is extremely important in this context as it sets the benchmark by which customers evaluate the value of the brand. To get its pricing right, brands need to understand what the areas are where the brand needs to overdeliver on value charged. When a brand delivers greater value or equivalent value to the price charged, its consumers do not feel that they are paying a premium. By overdelivering the brand stands to build a strong reason to buy and a great price value equation.

Brands charge a price for their offerings – be it products or services. This price is a source of revenue for the organisation and all brands would want to maximise revenue by charging a premium.

Brands do different things to get a premium over their cost of operation. This premium comes from enhancing the perceptual value of the brand. Innovations have helped brands earn a premium. Nike's Air sneakers provided a relevant innovation and the value of this was maximised by Nike's use of superstar Michael Jordan to charge a good premium for the product.

Even small innovations like a better grip for ball point pens, leak proof pens, etc. have seen brands getting a disproportionate return for the cost incurred. Consumers respond to relevant innovations often because they like the differentiation of the offering or find the brand is suddenly more relevant to their requirements.

Emotions have high financial value as many brands have found that consumers are willing to pay for prestige, companionship, reassurance, etc. It probably is a fair conjecture that BMW customers pay willingly for the emotional aspect of their owning what is arguably the world's finest driving machine. Similarly, customers willingly pay a premium for owning a luxury car like the Mercedes.

Florists often get a disproportionate return on the amount charged for the service of delivering flowers. They are able to earn a lot because the importance of getting hassle-free, prompt, reliable delivery of flowers carries a lot of value in the eyes of consumers.

Brands that contribute a part of their sales proceeds to a cause can and often do get a premium from customers that is disproportionate to the amount that the brand contributes to the cause. Customers often feel more comfortable with buying cause- related brands than actually contributing to causes directly.

Some brands restrict supply as a means of charging a premium. Knowing that only a select few own the brand makes customers willing to pay more to acquire the brand.

Brands that are seen to be providing a greater value than they are charging should be able to raise prices without losing market share and should therefore be able to get higher realisation and better profits. It is a healthy attitude to keep looking at how the brand can increase value provided and consistently push prices up without losing market share. Even if market conditions mean that a price rise may not be possible, it is healthy for the brand to have its customers feeling that they are getting more value from the brand than the value of the money paid for it as that will keep them loyal and make them refer the brand to others.

Pricing plays a huge role in enhancing brand valuation. The premium earned by the brand enhances the brand's valuation, and the premium not earned that goes into making the customer feel that they are getting good value for money works towards reducing acquisition costs, building loyalty and future earnings, all of which enhance brand valuation.

6

Your People Define What Your Brand Means

PEOPLE RUN brands, and strong brands have committed teams that work towards these brands' success. The greatest ally of a brand is its people, and their commitment is the brand's biggest strength. People are the driving force of any brand. People implement the brand promise made by brands, and therefore it is critical for brands to have the right people with the right aptitude and motivations working for the brand.

Avis fared well when it ran the 'we try harder' campaign, but the success was not just because of a brilliant line or positioning; it was because Avis actually was a brand that was built on greater striving from its employees and the campaign reinforced a truth that its customers saw and experienced.

Most organisations look at branding as a marketing function whose details are unnecessary for non-marketing staff. This is also probably why the number of truly great brands can be counted in tens and not in thousands.

It must be realised that motivated people can make a huge difference to the brand and the greater the number of motivated people working for a brand, the better it is for the brand. Everyone is important and anyone can contribute towards improving the brand. Take the case of someone working in the sourcing and materials department of an organisation – this person may be able to identify a new material that can make the brand offering more durable or lighter or stronger or less expensive in line with the brand promise.

Successful brands understand this and focus on their people. They have teams with a common of attitude and a sense of mission, and recruit the right kind of people with the right skill sets. The more evolved organisations understand the value of sharing the company's mission, vision and values so as to make all the employees of the organisation work together towards a common goal.

While most organisations understand the importance of explaining the corporate brand vision to its employees, the more evolved organisations take active steps to ensure that this vision is understood and internalised by all. It is important to ensure that all the different departments understand the brand mission, vision and values. This helps make sure that each department understands their role in fulfilling the brand's mission.

Brand missions can be motivating and uplifting to employees and in many cases help attract the right kind of employees who work with the brand for a long time. (A study states that 25 per cent of a company's employees stay on because they relate to the brand mission.)

Apple wanted to change the world, and all tech people knew this mission. Apple was able to attract many of the right kind of employees, people who valued this dream, and these employees were able to contribute hugely to Apple achieving its dream.

Sam Walton, Walt Disney, Herb Kelleher and Steve Jobs are leaders who lead by example. They simplified their brand's mission and made it palpable to their people. Creating a sense of purpose and excitement, they made their people work towards a common goal with purpose. These are brands where the employees work hard and play hard. The feeling of directly contributing to a meaningful mission brings out the best from employees working for these brands.

The direct impact of having motivated employees who believe in the brand mission and who understand their role can be huge.

With the number of customer interfaces with brands growing day by day, customers are increasingly getting to interact with the people behind the brand.

Customers meet salespeople, call toll-free numbers, discuss complaints with service people and send e-mail to back-office operators. Each interaction is a moment of truth and has a high impact, as customers tend to place great expectations on the human side of their interaction with a brand.

A customer may forget a problem with a defective tube of toothpaste but will not easily forget a rude call centre operator who makes fun of their complaint.

HR must recognise the role they play in recruiting, training and motivating people to work in line with the brand promise. It is not easy to motivate a large number of people to work together as a team, yet achieve individual goals and ambitions and HR plays a vital role in coordinating individual and corporate goals.

Many brands have not tapped the hidden potential of a highly motivated team and are more focused on getting the bottomline right without looking at the people who make the bottomline healthy.

The brands that do understand the importance of HR in creating a great, unified mission-driven environment lead from the front. Starbucks has been so successful in creating great brand experiences for their customers because their employees have been trained well and know exactly what they have to do to reinforce what the brand stands for.

For HR to reap the benefits of the motivated, united workforce, HR itself has to understand the brand promise with clarity. Often enough one sees HR not fully aware of what the brand stands for, and this can have disastrous effects on the organisation.

Knowing what the brand stands for immediately helps understand what kind of people are required for the brand.

A famous hotel brand in India offers hold efficient service as its clientele do not need the emotional gratification of warm, fawning attendants. The clients are extremely demanding and would prefer speed and efficiency to warmth.

Another hotel group, however, focuses on friendliness. The clientele of this hotel like being pampered and welcome the attention showered on them. Obviously, the attitude of people recruited for these different hotels would greatly vary. Clearly, the kind of training and KRAs for the front office staff of the two hotel brands would be very different.

Getting people with the right attitude is also important. Customer service people who enjoy interacting with customers and solving problems, salespeople who enjoy selling the brand promise, product developers who love creating as per the brand promise tend to last longer with the company and keep the brand promise alive.

The combination of the right attitude, aptitude and a deep belief in the brand promise makes for a successful brand that lives its promise because its people live its promise. SouthWest Airlines is a prime example of a brand that lives its promise because of its people. Disneyland is a wonderful place to visit because of the effort Disney employees put into creating a great experience. Harley Davidson is a strong brand because its people love the brand and their passion shows. Even their CEO is said to ride a Harley every day.

One of the most important facets of strong brands is the kind of culture that the brand has. Culture is about the way the brand goes about doing its business and operations. Culture is about how information is shared, the protocols involved, the level of formality and informality, the freedom of operating, etc.

WalMart, Infosys, Wipro all are examples of how brands can create a system of functioning that gets the best from their people and drive the brand promise. The longevity of a brand is linked to its ability to deliver on its promise. Its ability to deliver on its promise influences brand valuation.

The role of people impacts valuation directly and indirectly. The way great brands who have been genuinely caring towards their people have seen valuations soar shows that the right people playing the right role for brands can enhance the quality of brand experiences. These positive brand experiences help these brands attract and retain customers as well as employees. The decreased customer and employee acquisition costs and the high potential future earnings from loyal customers would push brand valuations higher.

The battle out there is tough, bloody and unrelenting. The more the committed soldiers a brand has, the better the chances for survival and victory. Building awareness of each employee's role in building /strengthening the brand and uniting them with a sense of purpose is as vital to victory as having powerful weapons.

7

Are Your Systems Protecting Your Brand?

A STRONG BRAND is always driven by powerful systems. The ability to make a promise and deliver on it consistently is what makes a brand truly great. Take the example of Coke: While it may appear that Coke's strength is derived purely through its image created by advertising and marketing, there are a lot of processes that go in at the back end that ensures that Coke can consistently deliver on its brand promise.

When Coke says that it wants to be an arm's length away from consumers across the world, a lot goes into making this a reality. Coke has to recruit the right bottlers, ensure sound distribution and create awareness and ensure availability of stock with retailers to make sure that the brand is truly available at an arm's length from consumers. And yes, this has to be done without any compromise in taste and quality across time and space.

In the case of Coke, there are innumerable areas that require diligent development of systems. Economical sourcing, rigorous quality control, careful selection of bottlers, aggressive distribution, scientific consumer behaviour studies are but a few of the several focus areas that require development of systems in order for Coke to deliver on its brand promise. These systems have to virtually become best practices.

Motorola has built its brand on the strength of its processes. Their Six Sigma standard is testimony to Motorola's commitment to its customers. BMW's claim to driving pleasure is manifested across millions of cars produced by BMW because the brand's engineering skills are a function of thousands of systems and processes working together across functions from sourcing of raw materials to state-of-the-art quality control to deliver on the brand promise.

Even a food product like hamburger that has several variables that can affect the offering can use systems to ensure consistency of quality the way McDonald's does.

The importance of systems is due to the fact that there is an implicit expectation of consistent quality from brands. Consumers expect one packet of Tide to deliver the same results as another packet of Tide. McDonald's customers expect to eat burgers that taste the same day after day without any variance in quality.

The ability to create high-quality offerings and sustain this quality across millions of units over years and across countries is what sets brands apart from labels. This is the result of a combination of a large number of highly detailed systems and rigorous adherence to these systems. McDonald's has perfected hamburgerology – the fine art of making burgers and goes to great lengths to see that these systems are followed. McDonald's Hamburger University is a great knowledge centre on systems that are to be followed by McDonald's franchisees.

At the core of creation of these systems is the need for a clearly articulated brand promise that defines exactly what the brand offers as this is directly linked to the extent of customer's expectations from the brand and sets the parameters on which the brand has to deliver. Branding is about perception management and brands need to set an expectation level and deliver in line or beyond the expectation level.

Having defined the brand promise and internally defined the level of minimum delivery that a customer would expect from this promise, the brand has to determine the systems that will make this promise come true and the areas that will drive customer satisfaction to greater heights.

Brands have to determine the areas that will deliver the brand promise optimally. Having determined the basic set of areas where the brand has to create systems that will create the minimum performance delivery, the brand has to then focus on the areas that will create a quantum leap in customer satisfaction viz the key values that drive the brand.

Having identified the primary and secondary areas of system development, the brand has to detail these systems to the minutest extent possible to ensure that each system is error proof and delivers consistent performance. Tests have to be done to see that systems run together harmoniously. Importantly, measurement parameters have to be put in place to ensure that the systems can be measured and improved.

These measurement parameters must have qualitative and quantitative components to ensure that the brand does not lose out on the intangible side which often is a blind spot in a purely systems-driven organisation. Employees need to be set KRAs that are in line with the various systems. Adherence to and improvement of systems must be monitored and rewarded.

It is important for the brand to monitor each facet of each system as an improvement in one facet can add to the brand's performance or have cost benefits. SouthWest Airlines apparently realised that by shortening the time to turn its planes it could cut costs by more than 20 per cent, so it geared up its entire team and operations to turn its plane in less than 15 minutes.

Great brands need to develop increasingly progressive systems that help the brands deliver higher levels of performance that ensure that their leadership position remains intact.

The belief in systems, the commitment to delivering the brand promise without exception, the passion to set higher standards, the vision to develop systems that provides cohesiveness to the brand promise are all symptomatic of brands with strong intent. It takes an amazing amount of work to develop systems for a brand like FedEx, but the blind faith customers have in the brand and its leadership position makes it worth the effort.

Brand intent provides the patience to ensure a 'monotonous' level of consistency. Intent also provides the energy to look at each microscopic facet that can impact the brand to keep pushing brand performance to greater heights.

Brands that are systems-driven are more likely to survive and thrive over time. When a brand valuation exercise is conducted the strength of the brand's systems and processes plays a large role in determining the true value of a brand. The oldest brands from the top ten brands in the world are possibly the best examples of how systems make brands endure and grow valuable.

8

Using Heritage to Maintain Meaning

WHEN A PRODUCT or service grows from providing beyond only functional benefits and provides a relationship, it becomes a brand. Brands have a heritage and the older the brand, the potentially stronger the heritage. This heritage is the trust, expectations and the implicit promise that consumers, trade and associates expect the brand to deliver on. The values of the brand based on which the customer–brand relationship is developed is an inextricable part of the brand's heritage.

It is important for brand custodians to recognize, respect and leverage their brand's heritage and ensure that it is maintained over the years. Brand custodians who ignore their brand's heritage run the risk of incurring the wrath of consumers and can expect to see their brand's ratings head south, for brand equity is linked to brand heritage.

The New Coke disaster is a good example of how a brand's heritage should not be ignored. The Coke values of being 'the real thing', 'symbol of America', etc. were dealt a harsh blow when 'New Coke' replaced the original Coke, depriving consumers of the Coke of their choice. Coke was strongly linked with the American way of life and when it was no longer available, consumers felt that something valuable was removed from their lives. As a result, consumers who had built a relationship with the brand based on these values felt slighted and showed it.

Consumers build emotional relationships with brands. They identify with brand personalities and relate to the values that the brands possess. When a brand changes the basis of the relationship or does something that is out of sync with its personality, it creates a dissonance amongst consumers who relate to the brand.

If Nike were to suddenly develop a spiritual side starkly in contrast to its existing image, consumers who love the brand for its strong aspirational side and aggressive 'Just- Do-It'-ness would probably feel deprived of the persona that comes with the brand. The absence of this persona (which rubs off on to its consumers) would probably not only erase the positive feelings towards the brand but may also create negative feelings towards the brand.

Similarly, if Harley Davidson were to adopt a 'wimp'-like stance, their consumers would most likely feel that the basis of their relationship with the brand has been violated. Customers who bought the brand for its persona will feel betrayed and their reaction is bound to be to the brands' disadvantage.

Domino Pizza's promise of service within the stipulated time or money back is a good example of how a practice became a tradition and has become a part of the brand's heritage. Ben & Jerry's donations to charity are well known and consumers associate the brand with its generous actions. If Ben & Jerry's were to stop this practice, it would take away a lot from what the brand stands for.

A brand with a well-documented heritage can tell its custodians things that consumer research may not. An understanding of its brand heritage will tell Coke's brand custodians to never pull out its main offering in place of a new offering as it did with New Coke, and this is something that consumer research may not reveal.

While brand heritage is not a substitute for consumer research and may not be able to predict consumer response to a new product or a proposed line extension, however, it can give a perspective to possible consumer response based on the past. This will help the brand custodian understand the nature of the challenge that the new product introduction or line extension poses.

The most important advantage that a well-documented heritage provides is possibly its most underrated quality. It gives brand custodians a sense of history and with it an increased feeling of confidence.

A brand's heritage could reveal some of the brand's intrinsic strengths, and this knowledge could be reassuring and morale boosting during lean times when the brand is under attack. It is always reassuring for the brand team to know that the brand has faced worse situations and lived to tell the tale. And if there are tips on how to counter this situation based on what the brand has done in the past, this information would be very welcome.

The perspective of documenting heritage for the benefit of future brand custodians is extremely important. Brands with a rich heritage tend to have high levels of morale. True and exaggerated tales of the brand's exploits are told with admiration and pride. Retailers and customers who have displayed extraordinary loyalty to the brand are remembered with fondness and tales of how the brand displayed extraordinary performance are recounted with awe and nostalgia.

At the same time, a well-documented heritage creates a feeling of history and makes brand custodians aware of the efforts put in by their predecessors. They also wake up to the responsibility that they have to make sure that the history and the predecessors' effort do not get frittered away. There is nothing like the burden of history to make brand custodians aware of the importance of maintaining and building on the years of trust that consumers have reposed in their brands.

GE has a huge record of its heritage with thousands of photographs and documents stored that depict events in GE over the years. This display of heritage which is open to the public also provides customers and the public at large with strong positive feelings about the brand. 3M has a well-documented history that shows how the brand has lived and grown over the years.

Not every brand has been around for a long time, and many brands that have been around for a long time have not documented their history. Brand custodians that document their part of the brand's history give their successors invaluable cues. Indeed there are several brand managers who are not conscious of the need to pass on a valuable heritage to their successors. Senior management needs to develop systems that ensure that this is done for the longevity of the brand.

Brand custodians must realise that they inherit legacies created/ enhanced by their predecessors and they have a role as the link to future brand custodians to document their part of the brand's history. The successes and failures both must be recounted with equal candour, and perhaps someday someone may make a huge success from an earlier brand manager's aborted plan.

Preserving heritage is important whether it is for a country or a brand.

9

Staying in Shape

PROBABLY the worst problems brands face are internal problems that hurt the brand by robbing employees of ownership, involvement and direction. Many brands with strong equity have collapsed due to people problems. These problems often are the result of poor organisational structure and poor focus. Delta Airlines in a cost-cutting spree closed some booking offices and reduced employee benefits. The result: employee morale plunged, and as a result of low morale, employees were not able to focus on customers. Customer dissatisfaction quickly set in that took its toll on the brand's equity.

Apple took quite a beating internally when it lost focus in the 1980s due to a lot of non-marketing problems. Engineers from key departments looked down on engineers from other departments. Frequent changes in plans robbed employees of security and focus leaving them feeling unsatisfied and vulnerable.

Frequent reshuffling of employee portfolios brings about a feeling of insecurity and often creates a mismatch between employees' core competencies and roles played.

Importantly, it causes an imbalance between employees' interests and inherent skills and the nature of their function. Lack of focus, unrealistic strategy, arbitrary shuffling of portfolios and frequent reorganisations can very quickly hurt a brand. As soon as employees or associates feel that the brand does not recognise them or that their role will take them nowhere, the relationship that they share with the brand starts getting eroded.

Many people derive meaning from the brand that they work for and the job they do, and being sidelined makes them feel that they have lost their importance. While those who have a long-term perspective may wait for their time to come, others probably will lose motivation, feel its impact on their performance and then move out.

A de-motivated team sends out a lot of wrong signals to external audiences. A large consumer goods company in India had a team with extremely low morale. The sales team used to continuously ask retailers of multi-brand outlets that they were servicing if these retailers knew of any vacancies in other consumer goods companies that serviced the same retailers.

The retailers consequently lost confidence in the brand and were scared that if there was an exodus of employees then quality and service problems might arise with the brand, which would lead to the retailer having irate customers. These retailers stopped stocking the brand and the brand slowly died.

Brands that have employees who care for the brand tend to weather these internal storms better. The employees' feeling of ownership and their pride of association often prevents them from walking away from the relationship, and they try to either ride out the problems or do something to correct a bad situation.

In the 1980s Harley Davidson was bankrupt and up for sale, yet no one wanted to buy this brand which had once enjoyed a cult status. 13 managers of Harley Davidson bought the company and revived the brand, which went on to regain its reputation as one of the world's most coveted motorcycle brands.

One of the most critical determinants of success of a brand is the level of pride and self-belief that its constituents have. Pride of association is a great source of motivation to make employees and associates put in their best for the success of the brand. This translates into excellence in a million tiny details that constitute the operations of the brand.

Pride makes employees work with unstinting commitment and prevents lapses in quality. Many employees derive immense pride from being associated with the brand they are working for and will do a lot more than required to see that the brand name is not tarnished. It raises the standard of work and discourages slackness or shoddiness.

Brands with proud constituents are often heard talking to prospects about how good the brand is. There is a persuasive ring to committed employees' tone when they speak whole-heartedly about the brand not because they want to make a sale, but because they want others to see how good the brand is.

A famous industrial products company in India ran a Rs 60 million campaign that told the world how good the brand was and the kind of high-quality products they had. This led to the sudden recognition and respect for the employees of the brand amongst external audiences. This acted as a shot in the arm for these employees who were good but not motivated enough to strive for excellence.

Now with a reputation to maintain, these employees improved all facets of their performance especially their dealings with external audiences in terms of timeliness, etc., so that no one would be able to fault their company in any way. The brand took a huge leap in productivity and ventured into a wide range of innovative new products that were only made possible because of the employees' new-found willingness to add to their reputation.

Pride is important for brands to steadily improve their standards, but self-belief is what helps the brand take bold decisions. Brands are like people – their actions are guided to some extent by their consciousness and self-concept. The Apple team of the 1980s were characterised by their belief that they could change the world with the Apple range of computers, and they did a great job with the Mac. SouthWest Airlines felt that they could create an offering that made flying affordable to people, and they have revolutionised the airline industry.

Proud employees have a feeling of bonding and unity to a common cause, which improves communication and leads to a reinforcement of a positive brand attitude. They look at means of improving areas of the brand's operation by discussing areas of improvement. Their solidarity helps them overcome any interpersonal differences they may have.

Brands that have employees with a high level of involvement and ownership tend to do better than others. Some brands try to buy this through stock options, but it has not always worked. In most cases, start-ups with passion like Apple and Virgin have been able to sustain the feeling of involvement, and this has led to a feeling of ownership. Microsoft with its high-value stock options has not really become a benchmark in terms of passion or excellence.

Employees who find their work being recognised and appreciated tend to be highly motivated and involved. These employees can do a lot in terms of voluntarily going beyond the call of duty and providing a better brand experience to customers. These employees stay loyal to the brand even when the brand goes through a bad phase.

Brands often use their heritage to build pride amongst employees. Knowing that they are a part of a highly respected company that has had several triumphs can make employees feel proud of the brand. Many people define themselves by the brand they work for and the more reputed the brand and the richer its heritage, the more this makes them feel proud of their association with the brand.

In addition to making employees look back on the brand heritage, HR needs to make employees realise that they are contributing to the brand's current achievements by showing them how their role and responsibilities help the brand in succeeding in its mission.

This will help the employees treat the brand's achievements as theirs. Brands that do not take the trouble to make employees feel that the brand's achievements are theirs stand to alienate sections of employees. These employees may feel that while the brand is growing, their own contribution to the brand's growth is negligible, and this could lead to disinterest and can work against the brand with employees either putting less into their work or leaving the brand.

Building pride and ownership is not easy, but the extent of benefits that it provides to the brand makes it something every brand must work on.

10

Every Experience Counts

EVERY TIME a brand's constituent comes into contact with a facet of the brand, whether it is an article in the newspaper or a call to the brand's toll-free number or usage of the product or service offering, there is a brand experience. Ensuring good experiences and consistency across brand experiences is critical for brands.

Brands are constantly on the lookout for means of improving brand experiences. Brand experiences that are lasting and impactful have a strong effect on brand equity and loyalty. After all, customer loyalty is largely based on customers having a good experience with the brand that leads them to want to repeat this experience.

Apple's customers find their computer usage experience with the Mac amazing and this experience makes them loyal to Apple. WorldSpace's customers find the clarity of reception and variety of content so rich that not only are they loyal to the brand, but they are strong advocates too. Dell's toll-free number provides educated, simple and expert advice on computers that gives its customers a good experience in line with what the brand stands for.

Brands that are experience savvy learn to continuously manage experiences. These brands are conscious of the importance of generating positive experiences as a means of building and maintaining brand equity and loyalty. Such brands try and build in components that improve the customer's brand experience at every stage. This could vary from information provided on the product packaging to specialised classes for customers.

Some brands pre-sell their offerings to make the consumer look forward to an enjoyable experience. Telling the consumer that he/she is in for a good time while consuming the brand makes consumers look out for a good experience, and that is half the battle won. Often this also works in conditioning the customer to notice and appreciate different aspects of the brand.

Brands that understand the value of creating positive brand experiences build experiential factors into the product or service offerings. A car rental that keeps the rented car waiting at a particular degree of heating or air-conditioning as predetermined by the customer helps the customer have a better brand experience.

Some cars use an air freshener that gives their cars a 'new car' smell to reinforce the pleasure of owning a new car. The 'new-car' smell is a good brand experience. An incense stick manufacturer in India features a picture of a popular deity on the pack so consumers are put in a religious frame of mind when they take the incense stick from the packet before doing their prayers. Sports channels use pre-match build-ups and post-match analyses of important matches to heighten the excitement and enjoyment of viewers.

Experience-focused brands research how their customers' brand experiences are. Some brands have realised that customers don't get the best from the brand because they don't know the best way to use the brand. Telling customers the best way to use a product or the best manner in which a service can be appreciated helps the customer get the best from the brand and therefore a better brand experience. This is why some brands provide elaborate details as to how to get the best from the brand. In fact some music companies sell music appreciation books, so customers know how to appreciate their music better.

While mass production can lead to a consistent level of product quality, there can be a lot of variation in delivery on the service side of the brand. Brands with highly motivated employees often create wonderful brand experiences for their customers – as a natural consequence of the employees' enthusiasm. Young brands are very conscious of the need to deliver positive brand experiences and put in a lot of energy in this area.

But brands need to keep this momentum going as they grow. Brands that understand the role of experiences in building loyalty and advocacy align their people and processes towards delivering consistent brand experiences. This starts with employees being educated on the brand mission, vision and values and the importance of manifesting these while providing brand experiences. Importantly, employees have to know the customers' expectations so that they can gear up to provide an experience in line with customers' expectations.

These brands set service levels for different aspects of customer – service requirements from speed of delivering information to speed of replacements. These brands communicate to customers about the time in which they can expect a query to be resolved, a problem to be fixed, etc., so that customers can set their expectations in place and get a more enriching brand experience.

These brands structure their organisation to see that customer–brand interfaces are managed well. Recognising the importance of consistently generating positive experiences, these brands put adequate resources to serve this purpose.

Using systems and customer information, brands can create systems to provide customised experiences. These experiences can be proactive or reactive. Proactive experiences are caused when the brand periodically looks at customer data and looks at ways in which it can create new experiences in line with the brand vision. Brands which don't have regular interaction with customers like sewing machines brands can look at creating interesting experiences for their customers through activities like setting up fashion designing classes, depicting excellence, modernity and versatility.

Reactive experiences are such as in the cases of brands where customers call in to their toll-free numbers. It is fairly common to have customer-care executives referring to customer details when they get a call from the customer and providing them with customised experiences based on the customers' relationship with the brand.

An Indian bank upgraded its technology and processes so that it could complete customer transactions in less time than normal. The bank decided that the time saved could be used for providing a warmer, more meaningful customer relationship. The bank went on to empower each branch to spend around Rs 5000 per month on initiatives that would help some customers get extremely positive experiences which would lead to advocacy.

For example, if the customer mentioned that he was busy and needed to courier a demand draft to another country, then the bank would volunteer to do so at their own cost (budget permitting) as a special case for the customer. The assumption was that with bank employees getting more time to spend with customers due to the reduced time per transaction, they would be able to know more to understand customers' needs and provide a better brand experience as a strong brand differentiator.

Brands need to audit the quality of experiences customers have with the brand. Brands need to also audit the experiences at each touchpoint and even create more touchpoints if the cost–benefit analysis works in favour of creation of such touchpoints. The key experience drivers should be identified and supported organisationally. Brand experiences drive loyalty and advocacy, and this is of paramount importance to brands.

11

Bullies Never Win

ARROGANCE IS one of the most disadvantageous traits that a brand can develop. Its causes are many, but it has only one consequence. Arrogance often develops when the brand's management feels that either the brand does not have significant competition or the brand's equity is so overwhelming that nothing will shake the brand's position of strength. They are so secure and confident in their own powers that they ignore customers and other constituents like employees, associates and sometimes even small investors.

British Airways is considered by many to have ignored the threat that Virgin posed for too long, probably because they felt that an upstart company could not pose a threat to an established player. British Airway's tactics in fending off Virgin were a sign of arrogance.

These tactics displayed a lack of respect for their customers' sentiments, public opinion and the law. The 'dirty tricks' campaign that British Airways launched against Virgin is well known. They called Virgin's customers and gave them misinformation about Virgin's flights so that the customers cancel their Virgin tickets and fly British Airways. British Airways showed great arrogance; not only did they not care about their customers' true preferences, but they probably also felt immune to retribution.

Microsoft has been accused of blocking competitors and copying competitors with impunity. Allegations of Microsoft trying to stifle Netscape and Sun dog Microsoft as the brand strives to look concerned about the commotion.

IBM has displayed arrogance several times. IBM's arrogance is probably not surprising because of its huge achievements. But because of this arrogance, they missed out on even greater achievements. IBM ignored the threat that Digital Equipment Corporation posed when DEC invented the mini-computer. When Apple came around with the personal computer, IBM again ignored them until Apple started posing a serious challenge. IBM went on to ignore Dell until Dell made huge stride in selling direct-to-customer computer systems.

The examples are numerous. Kmart ignored WalMart's steady growth. Kmart were confident that they had enough fire power and equity to outlast WalMart, but forgot that this was all based on their ability to serve customers well and give them great prices. The arrogant Kmart did not compete with WalMart because they probably felt WalMart did not have the pedigree to win over Kmart's customers.

Arrogance seems to be characterised by the fact that the leader brands are so confident in their powers that they cannot recognise or appreciate the brilliance of their competitors. 'If they have such a great product and its inventors are so good, then why aren't they working with us – after all, we are the biggest and best in this space,' said an employee of one brand that was being threatened by a smaller company's revolutionary new offering. The inability to take smaller competitors seriously enough has been a problem that has afflicted brands from the time the first cow was branded.

Few are immune to a brand's arrogance, not even customers. Some brands especially in the finance and consumer technology sectors do not take the trouble of educating customers. They keep speaking in a cryptic manner and indulge in tech talk and liberal usage of jargon to confuse customers into choosing them on the basis of brand name rather than on the basis of an educated preference.

In the absence of a clear idea of what exactly they should choose, customers decide to go with the biggest brand. It always seems to be a wise, safe and defendable decision to go with a big player especially when the subject is complicated. Customers assume that the biggest player is also the best brand. Customers reason that these brands probably are so big because they are very good, and their many customers are not wrong in their choice of brands.

Arrogance towards customers can take a more blatant form as in the instance of Coke. When Coke wanted to take Pepsi head on with the launch of a new sweetened version of Coke, they actually withdrew the traditional Coke from the market.

The withdrawal of the regular 'Coke', thereby dictating terms to customers, was a sign of arrogance. It seemed that the brand would dictate what people would drink by controlling supply. Did they think the customer would drink whatever they got under the brand Coke? Did they think they could ignore their consumers for long? Was it an attempt to arm-twist customers? There are various theories flying around amongst veterans of that era, but there is a unanimous feeling that it was a blatant show of arrogance.

When a brand is big, it tends to use its muscle to lean hard onto their trade associates. One doesn't have to be a victim of a heavyweight wrestler gone amok to appreciate that in any scenario it is unpleasant to be leaned on by someone much larger. Brands often have a love-hate relationship with the trade where they bully each other based on the market conditions, but in most cases, it is the big brands doing the bullying and occasionally making up through higher margins or increased support as the trade gets stronger.

Bullying trade is a common practice amongst several brands, and the presence of a strong competitor to the brand is probably the only way that trade has a chance to get back at the brand.

Brands are increasingly bullying employees by using a combination of high salaries and job insecurity to push them as far as possible. These brands have employees who are unable to resist the lure of a good salary and a respected brand name and who therefore allow themselves to be bullied. However, these brands do not have the genuine loyalty of their employees and their employees may someday harm the brand out of anger.

Some brands snoop on employees to ensure that no corporate secrets are being leaked. The continuous surveillance can be unwarranted and often is done with the confidence that in any kind of confrontation the organisation can prevail over individuals because the organisation has better resources on its side.

Arrogance hurts brands because it erodes equity. The constituents tend to feel that they are in an unequal relationship and this chafes. Over a period of time, the inequality and its unfairness erodes the relationship. It makes constituents want to push back against the brand, and this can only lead to a reduced valuation as the brand's ability to sustain / improve revenues in the long run get negatively affected. Not taking equity for granted or remaining paranoid is the best way to ward off arrogance.

12

A Friend in Need

PEOPLE TEND TO appreciate and remember others who help them in troubled times. They feel kind towards those who give advice and reassurance when things look bleak. This insight has important cues for brand custodians, after all, their job is to strengthen the customer–brand relationship.

Most brands don't look at helping consumers. They do not place themselves in their customers' mental and emotional position and empathise with what the customer is going through even if they themselves may be going through the same problems. But this could be an important lapse as brands are built in the mind and the mental state of customers could have a bearing on the brand. Brands have an emotional association with consumers and an opportunity to strengthen the bond always helps.

Let's look at some of the thoughts and feelings that customers experience during a recession. There is often a widespread sense of insecurity and gloom in an unhealthy economy. While some customers need to penny-pinch, others slash unnecessary expenses as a precautionary measure because of the air of uncertainty that prevails. There are a few things brands could do in this scenario, budgets permitting.

For example, brands can announce how they plan to fight retrenchment and actually add jobs as this provides much-needed good news. Brands can even look at sponsoring causes that help those who have lost jobs during the recession. The fact is that while this is only a small gesture, it actually can do a lot to improve the mood in a downbeat economy.

Importantly, it can inspire other brands to take similar actions. A CEO statement in the press that is motivational, like 'We are fighting to keep costs down for the good of our customers, employees and vendors in these troubled times. We will not retrench, we will recruit and fight our way out of this recession', would probably give heart to many.

There are many things brands can do to make customers feel good during a recession, and it is important that brands need to think of as many ways as possible to keep constituents' spirits buoyant and their thoughts positive. Different situations warrant different approaches – the focus being on making people feel better during a tough period. Media brands especially can play a large role in influencing public opinion and making people feel better and even guiding them on tackling such a situation.

Similarly, during a period of political instability – for example, following a state of hung parliament – brands can reassure customers about how this is only a passing phase and that things will improve soon. Brands with stature can use their leadership stance to comfort and reassure the public at large. They can provide the message that while things may be shaky on a political front, there is a good future ahead because people can rely on the business community behaving responsibly and with integrity in the nation's interest.

There is lot that brands had said and done after the twin towers were struck down. At a time when the world was shocked and saddened by the tragedy, it was heartening to see commercialism put aside and humanitarianism stepping out of the shadows. Many brands came forward with donations and aid for those injured and killed. This in itself showed a world united by feeling and served to build confidence in brands' willingness to support society and symbolised unity against terrorism, sending out positive signals across the world.

Even during wartime brands can help by sending out positive messages about how the war is progressing. They can post bulletins of those returning and set up help desks to help relatives of those missing.

There are times when the mood is sombre, such as the mood across the world and in UK in particular following the death of the much-admired Princess Diana. The wealth of emotion displayed showed a nation grieving and the world poorer for the loss of one of its few heroines. Herein lay an opportunity for brands to condole and share a few heartfelt words expressing their empathy with their customers.

Brands can communicate these messages in many ways without having to resort to high-decibel advertising. A simple message from the CEO to the press may suffice. Alternative, simple messages can be put up as sign boards at outlets where the brand is sold. Messages to employees, vendors and investors are also effective as these are important constituents of the brand and can disseminate information effectively.

An inspirational message will spread easily if it is believed to be spurred by genuine intent. It is important today to de-commercialise any message so that it is not seen as though the brand is saying or doing things only for effect. Brands that empathise with their customers will find customers empathising with them.

13

Use Every Opportunity to Brand

SALES IS the revenue earning area of brands. It is seen by many as a measure of a brand's success. Higher sales push earnings and profitability higher and create an overall feel-good atmosphere in the organisation with promotions all around and a sense of achievement prevailing across the company. Investors too are happy that their investment has delivered a good return.

With such quick tangible rewards, it is difficult for brands to ignore the desire for being sales driven. More and more brands are becoming obsessed with sales at the cost of their brand equity. With the pressure of hitting higher and higher, sales targets are driving brands to be frantic in their efforts. Brands seem to have lost the ability to be warm, friendly and helpful.

In the past brand marketers looked at every interaction with constituents as an opportunity to embed the brand a little deeper into the constituents' psyche. Unfortunately, today many marketers are looking at every touch point as an opportunity to sell. This has led to marketers trying to identify more and more sales touch points, and in the process they tend to intrude deeper and deeper into the prospects' lives.

The argument that they are giving prospects more and more opportunities to do what the prospect wants to do, viz buy the brand, is unconvincing and one sided. A counter-argument is that if the prospect truly wanted to buy the brand he/she would probably do so in most cases. It seems that it is the brand would rather not lose out on a sale than worry that the prospect will lose out on a great opportunity to buy their offering.

Providing information and earning constituents' respect is a dying art amongst many brands. As brands become more sales focused and less brand focused, a lot of subtle intangibles are disappearing, as also is equity.

As brands get more aggressive, they start ignoring values that hold many brands in good stead such as believing in customer privacy and freedom of choice. Some brands are virtually stalking prospects/ customers to sell to them. Brand information is handed out in a most miserly manner in order to make prospects approach the brand for further details, and then it is up to the sales team to convert these prospects into customers. This is often done through persistent intrusion of privacy and discounting by the brand.

By making prospects buy due to pressure created by an insistent salesperson or telemarketer, brands are showing almost a lack of belief that the brand can sell on its own merits and they seem to feel that if they provide proper information they will lose a sale.

Importantly, it also demonstrates a blatant disregard for the prospects' ability to choose a brand on his/her own based on perfect information. By hustling and giving spot discounts, brands stand to make themselves commodified. The lack of respect for the prospects' right to choose without sales pressure or freebies leads to the brand relationship degenerating into a price-based relationship. Often enough this could lead to a low lifetime value from a customer.

Customers who choose the wrong brand for their requirements have no one else to blame, but a prospect who has bought the wrong brand due to the salesperson's insistence can blame the error of judgement on the brand. If the customer makes an error of judgement on his/her own, there is no negative word of mouth and the customer may try the brand again under different circumstances. However, a customer who feels that he/she was hustled into buying will not give the brand a second chance and may even bad mouth the brand.

Sales-hungry salespeople can and have turned off many a customer. It is a worrying scenario for a brand when it gets a reputation of being a leech and pesters innocent seekers of information by badgering them to buy. Instead of attracting prospects, it will repel them. Selling per se is not wrong and is the lifeblood of any brand. However, it is important to ensure that buyers want to buy and do not have the brand unwillingly forced down their throats.

This sales persecution can turn prospects against brands as they try to avoid getting trapped by sales-hungry brands. These brands must realise that a situation where customers feel persecuted results in customers feeling that they are only appreciated for their money and for nothing else.

This diminishes the customers' value or self-worth, and no one would feel good towards someone who affects their self-image negatively. Brands also tend to hurt themselves in their attempt to sell by reducing their role in the consumer's life to only cost-effective convenience than having a larger emotional role.

An obsession with sales also prevents the brand from taking advantage of opportunities for feel-good small talk. Instead of just wishing customers a 'Happy New Year', many brands send out commercial messages along with their New Year greetings SMS. It is a wonder that some banks seriously think that there would be a large number of people who would be glad to hear at 11pm on New Year's eve that they are eligible for a personal loan at 1 per cent lower than the market rate.

Brands that are painstakingly trying to build equity are also blindly intruding on constituents without realising that this intrusion is counterproductive to their efforts at building equity. The fact that brands are losing perspective is worrying.

The fact that brands are thinking in a manner that is so oblivious to customer sentiments shows a worrying lack of perspective. There is invasion of privacy, intrusion, denial of information and badgering, all arising from the same source. Brands need to control their urge for higher sales and use their strengths to acquire customers. It is short-sightedness to try and use branding to build a relationship with constituents and then intrude on the constituents' privacy and abuse the relationship.

Brands obsessed with sales often put a lot of pressure on all the departments of the organisation. Production schedules are squeezed to produce in line with even hurried orders. Sales people and trade stand in danger of being overly glorified or censured.

Some departments are made to feel unimportant compared to the sales and marketing departments, and this impacts morale. The lack of perspective can cause havoc as employees forget the brand mission and target sales, even at the cost of quality and values. Favouritism abounds across employees and departments as systems, processes and values get undermined leading to an unstable organisation.

From a valuation angle it must be noted that while sales impact brand valuation, intrusion erodes equity and reduces the potential for future earnings, which diminishes valuation. An unstable organisation also has a reduced ability to earn revenues, again reducing valuation. But most importantly, an obsession with sales takes away its raison d'être, which is to fulfil its intent and that can be the single most debilitating impact on the brand.

14

Be Loyal to Earn Loyalty

BRANDS ACROSS THE WORLD lose billions of dollars every year because of the customers, employees and associates whom they lose. Brands keep losing customers and the valuable experience of employees and associates. Each form of loss can have serious implications for the brand whether it is loss of earnings in the form of sales or the loss of experience and its consequent costs when employees leave.

Acquiring customers is not easy and often comes with an additional cost. Some say the cost of acquiring new customers is six times the cost of retaining customers, and therefore there is merit in retaining customers as a cost-cutting tool. Besides, loyal customers tend to consume more of the brand than brand switchers and have greater value to the brand.

As loyal customers have experience in using the brand, the number of queries and service complaints often are lower. Lower costs and higher volumes make for greater profitability and that is the shortest way to any businessman's heart.

Building customer loyalty is the mantra for retention. While brands look at different means of building customer loyalty, they often end up missing out on the obvious. Loyalty is a two-way relationship. Consumers expect brands to be loyal to them and are automatically loyal to those brands that display their loyalty to customers. When a consumer realises that the brand has the consumer's best interests at heart, the consumer in turn places trust in the brand.

Some of the ways in which brands can express their loyalty is in terms of value, positive brand experiences and commitment. Brands that focus on giving customers value for money at all times often don't have a problem in terms of loyal customers. Brands can show their loyalty to customers by setting higher standards for themselves.

Brands that set for themselves higher standards than statutory requirements or competitive brands in order to see that their customer gets a better deal often have customers who display a higher degree of loyalty for the brand.

For example, Asian Paints in India is said to have an internal standard for their paint which is far superior to the statutory standard; so their paint is said to last longer without fading than it is legally required, thereby giving more value to the customer. The paint however, is priced on par with competition. Customers know that the brand is giving them good value for their money and has good intentions and would not want to move away from an equation that is working in their favour.

Brands that focus on ensuring that customers have a positive experience every time they interact with the brand can also be fairly certain of having a loyal customer base.

Using good material to ensure high-quality offerings, providing education on how to use the product so that the customer gets the best results, setting up toll-free numbers for easy access/ support, a quick and easy refund policy, good service, etc., all of these tools work towards delivering a positive brand experience, and every time the customer has a good brand experience, the brand's brownie points keep increasing. These brownie points would come in handy later in the event of an odd brand experience going awry.

Customers who feel that the brand is committed to them tend to reward the brand with their loyalty. Brands that keep adding improved offerings show customers that they need not look beyond the brand for solutions. Brands that evolve with their customers show that they respect their customers and want to keep up with their needs.

Brands that appreciate their customers are in turn appreciated. Brands that recognise and reward loyal customers find themselves being rewarded with loyalty, advocacy and at times even higher sales. Recognition and reward need not only be demonstrated through loyalty programmes but by the very fact that the brand is trying to do so much more for their customers.

Good brands keep looking at what more they can do for their customers – not necessarily how much more can they make out of their customers. Brands that want loyal customers have to focus on their customers. Economy brands should look at how they can build greater service at the same price or work prices downwards. Premium brands probably should look at how they can build greater emotional value into their offerings.

What most companies need to understand is that brand managers control the very basis of brand loyalty; programmes like customer clubs and other loyalty techniques aren't going to work if the basis of the loyalty is violated. Research indicates that over 30 per cent of customers appear loyal to a brand because of inertia, and this gives a marketing insight that if one does not give customers a good enough reason to shift, they won't. This means that just by keeping things constant a brand can retain customers.

While the fact that brands can achieve a lot just by being customer focused and by not shifting things around seems basic and fairly obvious. However, not many marketers follow this path. There is a lemming-like desire to change things around to get a few more percentage points of market share and this often can be disastrous.

Coke withdrew 'Coke Regular' to introduce 'New Coke' in a move that angered thousands of loyal customers. Volvo allegedly gave wrong results of a stress test. Cola majors in India are said to have sold colas with pesticide in them. Cadbury is accused of selling chocolates with worms in them. Each of these incidents has had an impact on brand equity and has shaken customers' confidence hurting loyalty.

Brands that try and cut costs by minor compromises in quality, brands that are deliberately a bit vague in their advertising, brands that set their billing system to round off bills to their advantage – all run the risk of being exposed as being disloyal and from there their journey is rapidly downhill.

Similarly, brands that are not loyal to their employees tend to see an exodus during bad times. SouthWest is said to be exceptionally loyal to its employees and avoided retrenching employees even when the rest of the airline industry was indulging in widespread job cuts. SouthWest's employees have been the backbone of the brand's success putting their might behind the brand and making SouthWest's promise of excellence at economy prices shine.

Brands with loyal constituents can expect healthy brand valuations as loyal constituents provide a good assurance that the brand has the resources and customers to ensure current and future earnings too are robust.

15

Concern Goes a Long Way

CONCERN IS one of the defining qualities of human beings. People display concern for others in millions of ways on a daily basis. The attribute of concern is recognised and appreciated by most people.

Brands need to have concern for their constituents – consumers, trade, employees, associates, investors et al and this is implicit in the brand relationship. Concern is a direct offshoot of the brand's intent. If a brand's intent is to provide customers with the ultimate driving machine, obviously this cannot be done without keeping in mind their customers' safety and respect for the customers' investment.

The more prominent a brand becomes, the greater the level of concern that the brand is expected to display. Therefore, a brand that wants to be seen as the ultimate driving machine would be expected to be environmentally friendly irrespective of whether the law dictates this or not.

'Concern' makes consumers feel that the brand will always look after their best interests. Concern is crucial to building consumer trust and lends perceptions of the brand being consumer friendly and accessible. Many consumers suffer from the 'small guy' syndrome and resent large organisations. Warm perceptions about the brand in the form of its concern help melt consumer resentment.

It is the consumers' belief in the brand's concern for them that leads them to buy offerings from big brands without apprehensions. Importantly, belief in the brand's concern can help tilt the scales in favour of one brand over another. It is common to hear customers saying something like this: 'An offering from P&G can be trusted. You just know they will make sure that a product has no harmful side effects and causes no health problems. They would have checked things out.'

There are cases where brands have made genuine mistakes, and the speed and fervency of their apology have made consumers forgiving, these unfortunate instances were handled well and did not erode these brands' perception of being concerned.

Intel's chip may or may not have been faulty, but still they were willing to take accountability and make good to customers who thought there was a problem with their chip. However, there are some brands that try to cover up their mistakes and lose credibility in the process.

Brands can manifest concern as a brand value in several ways. Rigorous product testing, quality control, toll-free lines, no-questions-asked return policies, etc. are but some of the standard features of most brands' operations. While these show for good marketing management, the benefits of these several operations can be nullified by brands' actions in non-marketing areas.

Big brands seen as employing child labour, brands seen as being unfair employers, brands using their size to bully associates, brands flouting environmental laws, brands cheating their investors, all lose out on the key value of concern. A common survey response is: 'If they don't care for their own people [investors, employees, associates, etc.] why would they care for us?'

Concern towards non-paying audiences is an important indicator of how truly a brand believes in the value of concern. Areas such as employee relations, investor relations and trade relations can therefore play an important role in helping brands build and maintain their equity.

More and more brands are now realising that brand equity can be damaged by poor decisions by finance departments, procurement departments, administration departments, etc., and not just by poor marketing management. The need to protect brand equity is the responsibility of every department. Every department would therefore need to manifest the brand's values, especially that of concern to their constituents, be they employees or vendors.

The importance of being seen as concerned cannot be overemphasised. Would consumers believe that a brand has genuine concern for them if they knew that the brand exploited its employees, bullied its vendors, polluted the environment, misguided its investors and bribed government officials? Surely consumers would believe that the brand is only paying lip service to them about concern in order to add a few more dollars to the bottom line.

It is therefore necessary to ensure that the value of concern is not merely a brand value but a management philosophy and that its manifestation is seen in all that the brand does.

Brands often associate with causes as a means of displaying how concerned they are. Brands that spontaneously associate with causes often score high on the concern ratings, and it is difficult to fault a brand that is known to devote time and resources to different causes. There often is a business benefit that arises as a direct consequence of brand 'caring'. It is not unusual to see a brand being rewarded for its concern with loyal customers, higher sales volumes or by getting a premium price over competition for the positive associations that the brand provides its customers.

However, not all brands are genuine in their concern and use concern as a smokescreen for defaulting on other areas. A brand that donates money towards poor children's education may at the same time be poisoning lakes with their poorly treated industrial effluents.

There is possibly merit in consumer activist groups' holistic research on brands to provide consumers with the true picture of different brands. This will separate the lip-service-oriented brands that profess concern from those brands that actually live and breathe concern for all.

Brands need to look at their actions holistically and see whether they are living their values properly and truly exhibiting concern. For by losing the image of a brand that has concern for its consumers, a brand loses an integral part of its brand equity.

16

Using Information to Determine Brand Relationships

THE CONSTITUENTS will require different kinds of information from the brand at different times. Brands that are ready to provide the relevant information show themselves to be responsive, responsible and transparent, and this adds a lot to their credibility.

But this is not easy, for this means that the entire organisation has to be aligned towards creation and dissemination of information. Understanding constituents' information requirements and preparing the brand's people and systems for organising and disseminating information is important. This involves empathy and understanding constituents' potential anxieties and balancing this with necessary levels of confidentiality.

For this to be possible brands must have a positive attitude towards information and decide on the nature and extent of information that can be readily accessible at different levels of the organisation and how much of this can be passed on to other constituents.

The importance of information lies in the fact that it helps constituents decide on various facets of their relationship with the brand. Investors get to decide whether they want to invest in the brand or not. Employees decide whether they see a long-term relationship with the brand. Importantly, customers and prospects decide whether they want to associate with the brand.

The customer–brand relationship has at least two important aspects to it. Firstly, the relationship comes with a cost to customers who pay to consume the brand. Secondly, by consuming the brand, the consumer is associating with the brand, and along with the association, there is an emotional relationship and this affects the consumers' self-concept.

Enlightened brands appreciate these two facets and develop their business processes around these. Respect for customers' decision-making abilities and their right to information is important for brands. Misinformation or lack of information could lead to an opportunity loss for customers, and this could lead to negative word-of-mouth publicity.

Proper information helps prospects make an educated choice on the relevance of the brand for the prospects' requirement, based on which the prospect decides whether to buy the brand or not. Buying the brand on the basis of information is taking a calculated risk that the investment in the brand will yield the desired result. The better the quality of the information, the lower the chance of the decision going wrong.

Prospects would want different kinds of information to help them in decision making from price to ingredients to manufacturing processes to comparative superiority, etc. The extent of information required for decision making depends on the nature of the brand being purchased. Understandably, a customer buying costly industrial equipment would want significantly more information than a customer buying an MP3 player would.

Brands that help prospects select the brand that is most relevant to their requirements are seen in kindly light. A small task of replacing a door in one's house could require answers to several questions such as whether to buy a ready-to-install door or a do-it-yourself door, where the doorknob and hinges will have to be fixed by the buyer.

Determining whether to use a doorframe made of wood, particleboard, medium-density fibre, high-density fibre or plastic is another decision that requires education, and the knowledge of the relative advantages and disadvantages of each material is necessary.

There are a host of other decisions that need to be taken, and the brand that provides comprehensive answers that help the customer take the right decision stands to benefit even if the customer ends up not buying their brand.

Brands that educate are seen as large hearted and non-mercenary as they show that they are willing to put the customers' benefit before theirs. Sometimes this means the brand has to provide category education and not merely brand education. Educating the customer so that they can choose the right brand for them and not necessarily the brand of the company providing the information shows a commitment to the customers' cause and this leads to positive advocacy.

Brands that educate their customers on how to use less of the brand and save at the expense of the company maximising its profits are seen as 'caring for the customer'. Telecom companies that help customers choose the optimum tariff plan, gas companies that help customers cut down their gas consumption, all show that they are committed to the customer beyond their own cause.

The willingness to lose out on some sales so that the customer benefits displays a brand's character and purpose. The willingness to educate shows a wealth of knowledge, and it is often assumed that a brand that knows so much about the category would have excellence in all aspects of its own operations.

Once a customer buys the brand, more information is required to help the customer get the best results from the brand. For example, it would be important for an air-conditioner consumer to know at what setting he would be able to optimise electricity consumption while getting maximum cooling, for this would help him get the best results. And the best results is what any customer would want having spent money on buying a brand.

But brands are more than products that conform to certain manufacturing specifications or follow certain benchmark processes. Brands have an emotional component to them and while it is important that the brand delivers functionally, it is also important that the brand does not let the customer down emotionally. Information on compliance issues such as the quality of working environment of those who help in producing the brand, the knowledge that workers are getting a fair salary for their work, etc. also are critical in constituents making the right choice.

The right to information lies not just with customers or prospects, but with other constituents too. Prospective and existing employees, investors, associates, the public, etc. have a right to know about the functioning of a brand. How the brand is doing is of concern to employees, investors and associates. Whether the brand is harming the environment or doing anything that is wrong is of concern to the public, and brands have a responsibility to provide this kind of information.

Brands that welcome constituents' enquiries and set up systems to handle these queries are seen as extremely credible. While a lot of information can be posted on the brand's website, a lot of information would need to pass through written and verbal communication and it is important to determine what information can be passed on and who can access it and how it can be disseminated.

Unfortunately, when there is a crisis and brands need to diffuse misapprehensions by promptly responding with prompt, accurate and detailed information, most brands clamp up and show the garrulousness of an oyster.

The more information a brand provides, the more it shows itself as being transparent with nothing to hide. The lack of skeletons in the corporate cupboard is quite a significant achievement and a strong boost to the brand's credibility.

17

A Brand's Character Determines Its Perspective

THE WAY A BRAND reacts to adversity and prosperity reveals its character. A consistent display of character by a brand over time creates a pattern that gets repeated over time building internal resilience. Not all brands have the strength and perspective to face adversity without losing focus or their core values. The ability to display perspective and character time and again separates the truly strong brands from the pretenders. The fact that many of the world's top 100 brands are over 100 years old is significant in this context.

In the course of business there are ups and downs and the values that a brand has guides it during tough times. In the early days WalMart often faced financial problems, but they never stopped their ambitious growth programme. Virgin Airways faced a long-drawn battle with the giant British Airways, but never backed down. SouthWest Airways faced many financial problems, but never lost their focus on handling short routes at super economy prices.

Brands encounter testing times frequently. It is always a cause for concern when a brand's sales are low. Even if a brand has enough cash reserves for the company to not have to worry about its survival, a significant drop in turnover is normally bad enough news for worry lines to start forming. A drop in sales volumes can be symptomatic of a larger problem and a sign of things to come, and it is a matter of maintaining perspective to get the right answers.

When sales are low, there is always temptation to boost sales through a quick-fix formula. A sales promotion scheme that offers a good discount or a 'buy one, get one free' offer can give sales a welcome boost; but frequent sales promotion schemes as a means of boosting flagging volumes is probably not always a smart approach.

Frequent sales promotions mortgage a brand's future for warding off the pressures of the present. When a brand conducts frequent sales promotions, it undermines the brand's equity and customers are not willing to pay the same price for the same brand. Often sales too start falling after a while as customers start entertaining suspicions of the brand's quality when the brand drops prices.

It stands to reason – consumer behaviour is learned behaviour and if a brand teaches customers to buy the brand at a lower price than normal, then customers will learn this behaviour. They would be averse to pay the normal price that they used to pay for the brand in the past. Customers also learn to look at the brand relationship from a price value perspective and not from an emotional standpoint.

Brands with perspective look at what factors have contributed to the fall in sales. If the market share has remained constant and the category sales have fallen due to a recession, these brands will not take any hasty decisions. Brands that realise that sales will fall or remain stagnant for a while due to a recession will look at how they can convince shareholders that this is circumstantial and not due to a drop in brand equity. These brands will resist pressure to compromise on quality or brand equity by discounting or any other initiatives.

These brands are also smart enough to realise that brands do not necessarily drive sales in the long run by dropping prices. Brands derive their strength from consumer preference. Brands that build an emotional differentiation have more enduring value. Discounting gives customers a rational reason to buy a brand.

Replacing an emotional reason to purchase with a rational reason to buy is a no-brainer as competition can always match a rational reason, whereas it is always tough to match a deep-rooted emotional preference. General Motors in the US is now seen to be looking at reducing rebates on its cars after the car industry has seen years of discounting and sales promotions.

Adversity also brings out the best from strong brands. Tough brands react to pressure with sound strategy rather than knee-jerk reactions. Brands that deliver a high value for money at a low price while maintaining their emotional differentiation have a sure-fire formula for success.

When faced with tough situations, successful brands focus on new processes, cost savings and adopt an aggressive attitude that helps deliver higher value to the consumer at the same price or the same value at a lower price. Harley Davidson improved their product quality and surged back into contention after being in a position where they were bankrupt and low on customer confidence. Pepsi had the courage to run the Pepsi Challenge live on television in their attempt to dethrone Coke.

Apple came back from a situation where it had huge inventory stocks, poor demand, no new products and a demoralised team to register consistent profits and growth. It would have been easy for them to throw in the towel as many other brands did, but strong leadership, committed employees and supportive investors saw them through.

In India there are three highly respected brands that were under fire. Pepsi and Coke have been accused of having pesticides in their soft drinks. Cadbury's chocolates were apparently found with worms in them. These brands faced a huge loss of consumer confidence and a credibility crisis. However, these brands seem to have overcome these problems and seem to be on their way towards regaining their earlier stature.

The ability to display character and focus on value provides the difference between success and failure. Tough times don't last but tough brands do.

18

Making the Bird's Eye View Count

THE CEO OF A COMPANY is also by default the company's Chief Brand Officer. Brand equity is the single most powerful asset of an organisation, and it is imperative that the senior-most person in the organisation takes complete accountability for preserving and enhancing brand equity.

There are exemplary CEOs who roll up their sleeves and contribute to their company's growth by involving themselves in all aspects of the organisation. Sam Walton used to constantly look at ways in which he could improve WalMart's performance whether it was by monitoring competition, educating his team members, working out better sourcing strategies, cutting down transport cost through better distribution or just raising internal morale. Jack Welch used his management skills to improve GE's performance.

By providing firm and fair leadership, CEOs build a lot of confidence in the brand. Constituents are confident that their interests will be looked after whether they are employees, associates, investors or customers. This confidence is critical as it boosts morale internally and makes everyone comfortable because they know that they will be treated fairly and that talent will be recognised and good performance will be rewarded.

Some CEOs consciously or unconsciously play the role of the Chief Brand Ambassador. They lend a part of their persona to the brand – Richard Branson's irreverence, Sam Walton's small-town wisdom, Lee Iacocca's charisma, Steve Jobs's intensity, all added to the brands they were handling and gave a little more to all those who came into contact with the brand than a faceless CEO would have. All of these CEOs also were able to handle the pressure of investors and deliver results without compromising on what their brands stood for.

One of the main roles of the CEO is to ensure that the brand delivers optimal returns on shareholder investment while ensuring that all the brand's constituents get a fair deal and grow with the brand. Investors have varying requirements – some focus on the short term while others look at the long term. The CEO has to ensure that short-term returns are not at the expense of long-term growth in share value and future earnings. This is not an easy task and investors make for impatient listeners.

CEOs that have a strong point of view and a clear direction for the brand are able to convince investors on the need to curb their impatience and greed while at the same time driving the brand to achieve the growth that investors would want. Smart planning, long-term perspective and a holistic perspective of branding helps build long-term value.

Importantly, they must also recognise the far-reaching implications of even 'non-branding issues'. While there is a lot of focus on the external, more public aspects of brand building such as advertising, distribution, etc., not enough focus seems to be devoted to the internal aspects of brand building.

A brand is an external manifestation of several internal processes of a company. The stronger the internal processes, the better the chance of the brand getting stronger. Time and lack of a continuous brand perspective can create pressures that damage the internal systems. Often enough brands fail because of 'internal haemorrhages' than because of external market forces.

There are a host of decisions that can affect the existence and future of brands. These decisions are not necessarily in the realm of conventional branding decisions, and CEOs need to look at these issues from the perspective of the long-term health of the brand. If not handled properly, there is the possibility of these issues eroding the brand equity.

Take the case of the Japanese, who financed their businesses in America with internal accruals and bank loans. Their financing route played an important role in helping build brand equity. The Japanese did not have to push sales to appease investors and could focus on building their brand value by focusing on quality and seeing that the customer got good value for money. As the brands did not have to resort to discounting and sales promotion gimmicks they were able to build a great deal of brand equity. This required a long-term perspective and a very holistic viewpoint.

Some seemingly innocuous areas such as sourcing and HR can have long-lasting and damaging implications on the brand. Brands that arm-twist suppliers or accept kickbacks from suppliers can get a bad name and suspicions of a possible compromise in quality are raised. Brands that employ child labour or that have poor working conditions in offsite operations too find that their equity is under attack with no defence available.

As the one person who has all the people and systems of the organisation at his/her command; the CEO is in a position to align all these resources to the mission of the brand and ensure that things are done in accordance with the brand's values, ethics and in accordance with the law of the land.

In order to get everyone to focus on the brand and the implications of any existing or proposed initiatives, the CEO should see that everyone who works for the brand – employees and associates – are aware of the brand's values, mission and the ethical standards that are to be maintained. This can be done in the following ways:

1. Conduct an audit on how existing practices are affecting the brand.

2. Ask for employees to mention in all memos/proposals how the activity/practice being recommended will impact the brand.

By doing the above, the CEO will create brand consciousness across employees/departments. Each employee will realise that there is a possible brand implication to his/her activities. Presumably, a lot of activities will be seen as truly having brand implications.

If a CEO realises that the company's growth lies in the growth of its brands then every decision must be made keeping in mind the implications on the brand. A company's CEO is its brand's foremost custodian and needs to recognise this role. The room on top is a room with a view; the more holistic the view, the better for the brand.

19

The Dark Side

THE PRESSURES of corporate life are many and varied. Some of these pressures are internal, based on individuals' personal ambitions and goals. These pressures can be driven by their desire for wealth, fame, power, growth, etc. Other pressures are work-related pressures where people are scared of losing their job because of the salary, security, etc., that the job provides. People react differently to pressure; some thrive on it, while others let it overwhelm them leading them to take morally and ethically indefensible decisions.

While it is easy to criticise wrongdoings, it must also be recognised that there are often strong motivators for misdeeds. The fear of losing a high profile job, the fear of one's failures being brought to light, the fear of being dismissed as a failure are real and frighteningly realistic. These fears are natural and get heightened under pressure.

Senior people who control the destiny of brands probably fall prey to these fears a little more easily than others because not only are the stakes perceivably higher, but these people are closer to the temptation of moulding things in their favour because they have the opportunity to do so.

Many people have a dark side to their personalities. In some, its presence is minimal; in others it is extant though its manifestation is strongly suppressed by the fear of societal repercussions and the individual's personal interpretation of morality. The desire to achieve, the fear of failure or the need to survive are often the reasons for the dark side emerging.

Brands are man-made and are also managed by people. The scope for the foibles of their creator or their custodian's dark side being imbued in the brand is immense. The manifestation of the dark side of brands is often indicative of the dark side of the people who control it.

The importance of the brand having an inherently strong value system is critical to each brand's existence as this forms the 'internal logic' that drives the brand's existence. Sound values born of an honest intent backed by a system of checks is the only way of preventing the brand from developing a dark side.

Walt Disney is an example of a strong man with a clear vision, an honest intent and sound values to back his vision and intent. The Disney brand today follows the guidelines set by Disney years ago. The brand is managed with strict adherence to these values and this has led to the immense credibility that the Disney brand commands.

With brand equity being a function of the brand's credibility and value system, equity can be quickly be eroded by a few misdeeds brought to light. And custodians are quickly realising that it is not merely poor product quality or other marketing faux pas that leads to diminution of brand credibility; that wilful misdemeanours in any aspect of the brand's operations can impact the brand negatively.

Inherent to the process of branding is the creation of trust that the brand will live up to its brand promise. Trust is the perception that the brand has the intent and ability to live up to its purported values and provide consumers with products or services of consistent quality.

The size of the organisation and its attendant infrastructure adds to the perception that the brand is equipped to continuously adhere to its stated values and deliver the requisite quality. The popularity of the brand serves as a statement of the brand's consistency in satisfying a variety of consumers over time.

The successful communication of the brand's values, the brand's intent and abilities lend to the brand relevance as well as brand differentiation aiding in the strengthening of the brand's equity.

A brand's non-conformance with acceptable ethical norms, as in the case of brand's indulging in dishonest business transactions or environmentally irresponsible acts are seen by the brand's constituents as a departure from the brand's earlier professed intent and values and leads to a breakdown of trust.

To these constituents, it signals the brand's movement away from earlier-stated values and in all probability the brand's commitment to its consumers. Diminution or modification of values in this light dilutes or revises the basis of the constituents' relationship with the brand and has an adverse effect on the brand.

The recent reports of how high-pedestal brands WorldCom and Arthur Andersen have lost a tremendous amount of brand equity following their misdeeds being brought to light testifies to how quickly large much-respected brands can be destroyed by non-compliance with consumer expected levels of ethics.

Importantly, the negative associations of a brand seen to be 'unethical' taint the consumer's brand experience and the consumer moves away from the brand to prevent further unpleasant association. Consumers often feel that a reduction in intent will lead to poorer quality of product and service and therefore a shallow brand experience.

When a brand is brought into existence, its creators need to create a code of conduct that is the charter of the brand. Checks that cover all the facets of the brand's transactions need to be established at the inception so that the brands' future custodians can protect the core of the brand – the basis of its trust. These values need to be a part of its DNA and therefore grow with the brand naturally over time and region.

It may be a worthwhile proposition for brands to create an independent trust that has the authority to supervise all facets that affect the brand. The trust will have to play more than just the role of an internal auditor but be a parallel brand custodian who will even have the powers to veto any decision if it is felt that this can affect brand equity negatively.

This is important as brand managers have their hands full with marketing-related issues and would not be aware of issues such as whether child labourers are employed in their offshore factories. The presence of an independent trust that is responsible to safeguard the brand's equity will possibly be a good move as it is seen that brand equity is the single most valuable asset of many companies exceeding even the value of all their fixed assets, so guarding this is of paramount importance.

The Dark Side can be dominant and terrifying. It can cause untold misery and thrives on the weakness of man. Preventing the Dark Side from surfacing is a worthy effort for man or brand.

20

Carry Your Size with Care

BIG BRANDS tend to have a problem because of their size. For all the obvious benefits that come with size, there are often a fair share of problems too. Big brands are often seen as greedy and unscrupulous and many people easily believe allegations made against these brands for no other reason than the fact that these brands are big. There are enough stories of big brands who have adopted unscrupulous means to justify a certain distrust towards big brands.

Some individuals are prickly when they interact with large organisations. Perhaps it is the bigness of these organisations that makes these individuals whether customers, investors, trade or associates feel especially small. Brands need to recognise this and take preventive action.

Brands need to carry their size with grace and not intimidate customers. The immediate problem for most brands is the fact that they are structured in a manner that prevents their constituents from having easy access to key people when they have a problem. The apparent facelessness of the organisation makes brands seem impersonal money grabbers with no loyalty or sense of responsibility towards their constituents.

When the going is good, customers, small investors, employees, associates, trade, etc. are glad to associate themselves with big brands for all the stature and emotional satisfaction that the association provides. It is normal for many people to root for the underdog and boo the favourites. However, the same people often prefer to try to transact with the big players, for big brands inspire confidence whether it is in terms of product quality, financial stability or any other parameter. But when the constituents' trust is misplaced, then suddenly the brand has to contend with the fury of constituents who feel betrayed. This often is an avoidable problem.

In the process of growth, brands tend to structure themselves in compartments in an attempt to ensure that every employee is able to work with focus and maximise productivity. Often this involves employees focusing on a single function and a single department. Responsibility and authority are restricted to a single department.

Not all problems can be solved in this manner and often interdepartmental interaction and cooperation is required. The lack of smooth interdepartmental coordination and requisite decision-making authority leads to a distance between the organisation and its constituents.

The fact that often bureaucracy makes the organisation unable to comply even if it wants to leads to greater frustration. The aggrieved parties could be as varied as a small investor who wants details of his/her dividend or a customer who wants information on the refund policy on faulty products or even an employee who wants clarification regarding his provident fund withdrawals.

But what may be a small irritable complaint from a constituent can spark off disproportionate resentment. The latent dislike for big brands comes to the fore and everything goes to build and reinforce the case that these organisations are not interested in the constituent.

Once this feeling sets in, the constituent starts taking credit for solving the problem in spite of the brand and not in conjunction with the brand. The negative talk starts about the brand and this makes more people develop an aggressive/offensive attitude towards the brand.

In such a scenario only those constituents who have little or no direct interaction are happy with the brand, while a few with problems are unhappy and tend to make martyrs of themselves to the cause of spreading ill-will towards the brand.

Genuine mistakes also tend to be viewed with suspicion when committed by a big brand. An error in supervision that leads to a bad batch of medicines being released into the market can be misconstrued by people because of their latent antipathy towards big brands. When cola majors Coke and Pepsi were found to have a higher-than-permissible level of pesticide content in their colas in India, many viewed it as the doings of large MNCs who felt that they were above the law. Others felt it was a lack of concern or just plain apathy. Not many saw it as a genuine mistake.

Big brands tend to complicate matters further by their cloak and dagger acts of maintaining extreme secrecy. 'The more you hide the more of your character you reveal' is the saying that comes to mind. A look at the terms of contracts that brands sign with employees and associates would make anyone suspicious. By exercising undue secrecy these brands make people think that there are skeletons to be found if and when the sniffer dogs are released.

Brands need to be conscious that they can easily cause resentment because of the size and structure. Therefore brands must create interfaces that ensure warm, friendly interactions and speedy resolution of problems. They need to be conscious of the impression they create and work towards making the brand be seen in a kindlier light.

Richard Branson's antics and his easy accessibility to his constituents has made sure that the Virgin brand never seems distant or impersonal. Sam Walton's strong small-town culture and the stories of the friendly WalMart culture have a disarming effect on its constituents.

CEOs who are known to possess strong integrity, are accessible and display genuine intent can prevent their brands from getting a negative image. Such CEOs tend to have fewer brand problems. CEOs who take the time to reply to customers' mails and meet their constituents can give the brand a reputation of being genuinely constituent friendly.

It is unfortunate that many people have biases against big brands, but it is human. It is wise to recognise this and nullify a negative image before it can build. A negative side, however small, is like a ticking time bomb that can go off at any moment.

21

Building Brands, Building Meaning

AS EXPLAINED in earlier chapters, the process of branding is the process of building meaning into an offering. Through branding one adds meaning to a logo, a name, a job, etc. The word Coke means a lot more than just the name of a brownish black-coloured drink. The name Pepsi is almost laughable as a word without the brand image attached to it. Fanta, 7Up and, Dettol mean nothing as words, but they mean a lot as brands.

Meaning is what constituents derive from the brand beyond the functional offering of the brand. The feeling of satisfaction from contributing to keeping the world's environment safe may be the meaning that a Greenpeace employee gets from his association with the brand. This goes beyond the functional association of working for this organisation for a living. Similarly, the meaning that a BMW owner gets from the brand is built around the pleasure and pride of driving the world's finest car, which goes beyond the mere functional benefit of a car that is capable of achieving a certain engine speed and a particular fuel efficiency.

Brand meaning gives people added reasons to associate with a brand and makes the association with the brand more fulfilling. The act of consuming a brand can have several meanings. Consuming Coke may connote an appreciation of the American way of life and endorsement of a brand that is uniquely associated with the growth and evolution of the United States of America.

Many brands have developed more meaning than merely their product meaning. To some people supporting a brand is about supporting a way of life as in the case of those who buy The Body

Shop's products. Some brands stand for supporting a cause just as avoidance of a brand signifies shunning a cause. Some brands symbolise the hard side of capitalism like GE, while other brands like Ben & Jerry's represent the softer side of business.

Brands stand for many more values than just those that they advertise and these add greater definition to the meaning of the brand. Brands can reflect good ethics, the triumph of ingenuity over size, that it is possible to be ethical and successful at the same time, and much more. All the values that a brand stands for directly or indirectly add meaning to the brand.

Meaning stems from the brand's intent and values. By adding meaning, brands become richer in terms of imagery, experience and emotion. Without meaning brands are pallid, lifeless and nondescript. By adding meaning brands come to life and pass meaning on to all that they touch – investors, employees, consumers et al.

Meaning sets the basis for relationships as people want to have relationships with live vibrant offerings and not with functional offerings. Constituents develop expectations and aspirations around this relationship and the relationship gains involvement.

It is these relationships with customers, prospects, trade, etc. that provide brands with the business benefits of sales, higher realisation of value, reduced acquisition costs due to customer and employee loyalty, etc.

Every act of a brand adds or reduces its meaning. If the brand's act is positive, it adds positive meaning to the brand and strengthens existing relationships and attracts new constituents. If the brand's act is negative, it creates negative meaning to the brand and diminishes relationships and repels new constituents from forming a relationship with the brand.

Every time a brand does an unethical act, it reduces or changes the meaning associated with it, therefore losing a part of its relevance to investors, employees, customers and associates. This can hurt the brand as a business.

It is therefore vital, even for greedy brands, not to do unethical, inconsiderate acts such as bullying employees or vendors, using child labour or being environmentally unfriendly, despite the short-term business benefits that these acts offer. These acts of the brand will ultimately be counterproductive by reducing brand meaning and hurting the brand financially in the long run.

The message is simple and clear: The more positive relevant meaning brands build for themselves, the longer they stand to last as profitable strong businesses. Brands with meaning like Coke and Pepsi, which are over a 100 years old have tremendous financial strength and are extremely attractive as businesses thereby showing the business merit in building positive relevant brand meaning.

Many first-generation brand owners have seen visions of what their brands could do and went on to give the world brands that are financially, culturally and socially significant. It is for those involved in starting and running brands to decide what they will pass on to the world.

Brand meaning comes from custodians with character, ingenuity, vision and humanity. It touches the lives of all it comes into contact with and there is no a better tool for creating and spreading economic and social value than a brand with meaning.